Pacesetters

Setting the Standard, Not Following the Trend

Benny Perez

WinePress Publishing Mukilteo, WA 98275

DEDICATION

To Jesus, the one who believed in me and always will!

To my loving parents Jess and Carol Gutierrez who set a standard for me to follow. You bucked the trends of the day to give me a goal to strive for. I will do my best to be the Pacesetter you said I would be.

To my family who is always just a phone call away. You have affected my life more than you think.

Also, to my best friend, Iann Schonken, who continued to believe in me even in the rough times. Your life is a true example of a Pacesetter. Thank you for running with me.

ACKNOWLEDGMENTS

My thanks and gratitude go to:

Jesus Christ for setting the pace for all to follow;

Ken Squires for letting a dream become a reality;

Billy & Pam Farrar who pushed me to higher heights;

Doug Shafer for the extensive work in helping write the book and for carrying the same vision;

Doug Healy, Ken Ewing, Paul Garcia, Dave Schaal, Iann Schonken and Jon Martinez for helping set the pace;

My youth workers at Marysville First Assembly for all your work and helping a dream become a reality;

TC^2 Youth Ministries, the greatest youth and youth church in America. You have proven that Pacesetters exist in the youth culture today;

Chuck and Athena Dean for all your effort in such a short time;

Cindy Klein for proof reading and encouraging.

CONTENTS

Chapter One

The Trends

> *"Satan is not intimidated by the shouts and boasts of believers who do not have an intimate relationship with Jesus. He knows that as long as darkness reigns unchallenged and unconquered in many areas of their own lives, those believers pose no real threat to his kingdom. Jesus is the One whom Satan fears. If believers are not filled with the reality and knowledge of Christ, Satan knows it is only a matter of time until they will become victims, not victors."[1]*
>
> From "Passion for Jesus"
> by Mike Bickle

We are in an age when there seems to be an outbreak of evil and corruption. The trends seem to be pointing to a world gone mad. You may ask what kind of trends am I talking about? Consider the following statistics of what happens everyday in America, the country that is supposed to be one nation, under God, indivisible, with liberty and justice for all:

- **1,000** unwed teenage girls become mothers
- **1,106** teenage girls get abortions
- **4,219** teenagers contract sexually transmitted diseases
- **500** adolescents begin using drugs
- **1,000** adolescents begin drinking alcohol
- **135,000** kids bring guns or other weapons to school
- **3,610** teens are assaulted; 80 are raped
- **2,200** teens drop out of high school
- **6** teens commit suicide

These are not statistics that are limited to one segment of our society. These are the events that are effecting every facet of the American society. It is reported that juvenile crime is soaring and it's going to get worse.[2] We read of cold-blooded kid killers who are murdering and having no remorse. One teenage offender upon hearing that he might be charged with murder exclaimed, "Hey, great! We've hit the big time!"[3]

Many people may say that only secular society is effected, and the church is doing much better than that. However, we must come to grips with the reality of what is actually happening. In my years of ministry, I have seen trends of the culture influencing the church instead of the church influencing the culture. One time a young person came to me and asked if they could organize a Christian dance at our church. They wanted to have a DJ and hot Christian music so they could invite their non-Christian friends to be a part of the evening. I lovingly said "no" and encouraged them for having a heart that wanted to reach the lost. I assured this person that what the world needs is a radical encounter with the living Christ. What was needed was something so different that their friends knew that God was alive.

The culture is seeping into the church and the ones that are paying for this trend the most are the Christian youth in America today.

Josh McDowell in his book, *Right from Wrong*, makes the following statements:

> *"Large proportions of our youth—a majority of whom say they have made a personal commitment to Jesus Christ—are involved in inappropriate, immoral, even illegal behavior. The data show that young people from good Christian homes are succumbing to the pressures of our society."*[4]

The statistics are staggering and heartbreaking as we notice trends within the church. Young people have told me "Pastor Benny, it is not that bad." What they are telling me is that it is bad, but not nearly as bad as what is happening in the society around them. Are we making excuses for the trends that are hitting our churches? How about our personal lives and those of our families? Now is the time for people to rise up in the power of God to change the trends and bring standards back again to the world and to the body of Christ. Now is the time for each of us to become *pacesetters*. We need to move out in front and set the pace for the future generations to follow.

In the Bible we see a story of a young boy who becomes king. The boy's name is Josiah, which means the fire of God. Josiah becomes king of Judah when the nation was filled with idolatry, witchcraft, murder, immorality and all manner of heathen practices. Instead of the Word of God, the society had seeped into the very fiber of the lifestyles of the people. The trend of the day required a Pacesetter to come to the forefront. This was the perfect time for Josiah to come into the picture.

In 2 Chronicles 34:1-3, we read of Josiah becoming king of Judah. However, this was not the first time that Josiah is mentioned. Josiah and what he would do is prophesied in I Kings 13:2. God knew 322 years before Josiah was born what his destiny was going to be. God looked into the future and saw the need for a Pacesetter. In the book of Ephesians 2:10 we read:

"For we are God's workmanship created in Christ Jesus for good works, which God prepared before- hand that we should walk in them."

God has a plan for you to fulfill that no one else can fulfill but you!

Josiah was God's person to bring about the standard in Judah once again. We read that Josiah became king at 8 years of age. He reigned for 31 years and did not turn to the right or to the left but he kept his focus straight on God! Josiah was not going to follow the trends of the society around him, but was going to make a change—He was ris- ing up to be the Pacesetter—Setting the Standard not Fol- lowing the Trend.

There are some important traits of a person who begins to set a new standard. Let's examine Josiah's formula for being a Pacesetter.

1. He knew he had to pray. 2 Chronicles 34:3

The Bible says that while he was still young, he began to seek the God of his father, David. Josiah had a burning desire to know God as much as David knew God. I can imag- ine Josiah reading the stories of how David was a mighty warrior who slew giants and captured cities. Josiah knew that the secret of David's strength was communion with God. Therefore, Josiah knew that the way to know God was to spend time in prayer.

10

Prayer is literally when we, as finite people, begin to speak with an infinite God. E. M. Bounds wrote, "That Satan trembles when he sees the weakest saint upon his knees."[5] Josiah knew that his power to effect his nation would begin in the prayer closet. He also knew that you are never to young to get serious about God. As people who want to begin to change the trends, let us, like Josiah, be people who begin to seek God. Jesus is the only one who can change the tide that is sweeping our land and so we must begin to march as soldiers on our knees.

2. He took action concerning his convictions.

Josiah did not simply stay in his prayer closet, but put a plan to his prayers. At the age of 20, he began to purge Judah and Jerusalem of the "high places." All the witchcraft and pagan religions were cleared out of the temples and countryside. Josiah had the fire of God burning inside of him that compelled him to bring change. Josiah knew that he could not do everything, but he knew he could do something. Josiah was a man that began to lead others by example. We can do the same thing in our day and our hour. As ones called to raise the standard, let us make the same commitment as Josiah did—one of ACTION!

As a pastor I was challenged one night not only to pray for the youth of my city, but to go out and reach them. As I was driving down the main street, my heart broke as I saw literally hundreds of youth lost without Jesus. I began to pray that the Holy Spirit would begin to pull them into church. However, that was not good enough, God wanted to do more. I was challenged by the Lord to go out to the streets and talk with the youth. We started Friday Night Invasion where I and fifty other students would hit the streets to share our faith. I challenged our youth with the need to put action to our convictions. As a result of our efforts, we saw many youth come to know Christ. We began to change the trend in our city on Friday nights from cruising in cars to cruising for Christ. The result was an explosion of boldness and tremendous growth within our youth church.

3. Josiah was honest about sin.

Josiah was honest about his own life and how it had come short. We read that he tore his robes when he heard the Word of God. Josiah had realized that he had been coming up short with his lifestyle and he wanted to do something about it. We, as people wanting to change the trends, must get honest about our lives and how they are measuring up to the Word of God.

You see, Josiah knew that sin had to be dealt with because sin is a killer. The Bible states the wages of sin is death, both physical and spiritual. Anytime we have sin that is in our lives we will pay a price. We must be quick to repent and confess so that cleansing might occur. We read in I John 1:9:

> *"If we confess our sins, He is faithful and just to forgive us our sins and to cleanse us from all unrighteousness."*

To confess means to agree with God that our actions are wrong and that we must turn away from them. Josiah knew that in order to bring change that he needed to be honest with his sin and the sin of the people. In order for us to see radical change, we must do the same thing.

Less than 100 years ago there was another young man who was not afraid to get honest about sin. This man, Evan Roberts, had a profound experience with God in which he experienced cleansing and awakening in his own life. Roberts began preaching that people needed to confess any known sin to God. They needed to make right any wrong done to man, put away any doubtful habit, and obey the promptings of the Holy Spirit. Within three months a hundred thousand converts filled the churches of Wales. Roberts was not afraid to call sin by its name. He was a man who got honest about sin in his life and challenged those around him to do the same. The result was a changing of the trends and the setting of a new standard. Evan Roberts became a *pacesetter*.

4. Josiah rediscovered the Word of God.

During Josiah's reign, the book of the Law was discovered. Josiah now came face to face with what the Lord required of His people. For the first time, Josiah began to realize how far the trends of his time had taken the people away from serving the true God. When we discover the Word we realize how far we, as a people, have strayed away from God.

In America we must realize that we were founded upon the Word of God. Note what one of our early forefathers, James Madison, said:

> *"We have staked the whole future of American civilization, not upon the power of government, far from it. We have staked the future of our political institutions upon the capacity of mankind for self-government; upon the capacity of each and all of us to govern ourselves, to control ourselves, to sustain ourselves according to the Ten Commandments of God."*[6]

It was the intent of our founding fathers to have this country founded upon the Word of God and to continue to be governed by the Word Of God. Patrick Henry, the great patriot, stated:

> *"It cannot be emphasized too strongly or too often that this great nation was founded, not by reli-*

gionists, but by Christians, not on religions, but on the gospel of Jesus Christ."[7]

The trends in America have been changing drastically in the last thirty years. In 1962, the Supreme Court ruled the following prayer illegal:

"Almighty God, we acknowledge our dependence on Thee, and we beg Thy blessing upon us, our parents, our teachers, and our country."[8]

The courts continued the trends again, ruling in 1967 a poem illegal that was directed towards God. Our nation has slowly gone the road furthest from the Word of God. In 1980, the Supreme Court ruled against the posting of the Ten Commandments:

"If the posted copies of the Ten Commandments are to have any effect at all, it will be to induce the school children to read, meditate upon, perhaps to venerate and obey the commandments ...This...is not a permissible state objective under the Establishment Clause."[9]

These are the trends that are happening in our nation but it does not have to effect the church. We in the church, like Josiah, have to rediscover the Word of God again. It will tell us the way to live and how to do it. It is a time for Pacesetters to be raised up within the churches of America again.

5.   Josiah called others to come with him.
Josiah knew that he could not change the trends by himself; he needed to enlist other people to help him. What is happening in our world and churches is too big for one per-

son to bring change. God is calling the whole army to rally to the call of a higher standard. We read in 2 Chronicles 34: 32 that Josiah had everyone pledge to follow the Word of the Lord. After Josiah rediscovered God's Word, it changed him. The change in Josiah effected him so much that it naturally began to effect the ones he had influence over. Notice what Josiah did:

"Then the king stood in his place and made a covenant before the Lord, to follow the Lord, and to keep His commandments and His testimonies and His statutes with all his heart and all his soul, to perform the words of the covenant that were written in this book..." 2 Chronicles 34: 31.

It reminds me of what happened here at TC² Youth Ministries of Marysville First Assembly of God. In the spring of 1992, God called me to come to the great Northwest. I was working at the time in Apple Valley, California, as a youth pastor. The phone rang one day and on the other end was Ken Squires, who was becoming Senior Pastor of Marysville First Assembly. He asked me over the phone to become the youth pastor of his new church. I can remember asking him where in the world was Marysville, Washington? I knew God was getting ready to move me, but I thought it was to the limelight not the moonlight of Marysville. But God had other plans because significant movements start in small places.

After taking the position, I realized I had inherited a youth ministry of 20 students. The majority of them were cold and apathetic to the things of God. I wondered what was God doing to me and if He had made a mistake. However, the Lord knew that the students were Pacesetters who only needed someone to call them to Set the Standard and Not Follow The Trend! I began to do just that, and the students began to respond. The radical call to commitment brought radical change to a ministry and a city.

The first year we saw our youth ministry grow to over 100 students. The power of God was so evident as we saw lives touched and changed.

The students began to learn the principles that Josiah taught his people:

Here's what they learned:

1) They knew they had to pray.

2) They became activists. They took action concerning their convictions.

3) They became honest about their sin and confessed it.

4) They rediscovered the Word of God and began to live by it.

5) They called others to join them in following Christ.

The results have been nothing less than miraculous. The youth ministries of Marysville First Assembly of God has exploded into a movement that is impacting a county, and influencing the youth culture. At present, the youth church has grown to 500, with meetings on Tuesday and Wednesday nights. We have realized that by a few calling a few, who continue to call a few more, very quickly a great movement can be built.

The key to remember is that it is Jesus, the ultimate Pacesetter, who is the One who receives all the glory. We must do our part to continue realizing who we are in Christ so that we have Christ's power flowing out of our lives. In fact, the next chapter will deal with the subject of identity, one of the keys characterizing a *Pacesetter*.

1. Mike Bickle, Passion for Jesus, (Orlando: Creation House, 1993), p. 154.
2. Ted Gest, "Crime Time Bomb," U.S. News & World Report March 1996: p. 29.
3. Josh McDowell, Right From Wrong, (Dallas: Word Publishing, 1994), p. 4.
4. Ibid, p. 8-9.
5. The Complete Works of E. M. Bounds on Prayer, (Grand Rapids: Baker Book House, 1990), p. 344.
6. "Separation Between Church and State: The Truth," (Boise: Grapevine Publications, 1992).
7. Ibid.
8. Ibid.
9. Ibid.

Chapter Two

Who Are You?

> *"He is the one who can tell us the reason for our existence, our place in the scheme of things, our real identity. It is an identity we can't discover for ourselves, and others can't discover in us—the mystery of who we really are. How we have chased around the world for answers to that riddle, looked in the eyes of others for some hint, some clue, hunted in the multiple worlds of pleasure and experience and self-fulfillment for some glimpse, some revelation, some wisdom, some authority to tell us our right name and our true destination. But there was, and is, only One who can tell us all this: the Lord Himself."[1]*
>
> From "Clinging—The Experience of Prayer" by Emilie Griffin

Shortly before His triumphal entry into Jerusalem (which would end a week later with his crucifixion,) Jesus was having a conversation with his disciples. By now Peter, John,

Andrew and the others knew Jesus quite well and had come to expect these teachings as they traveled from village to village. On this occasion, as they entered the region called Caesarea Philippi, Jesus asked all of them this question: *"Who do people say the Son of Man is?"*

The disciples reported that some people thought Jesus was John the Baptist raised from the dead; others thought maybe he was Elijah or Jeremiah. Jesus looked intently at the men who had shared his meals and ministry for the past three-and-a-half years and said, *But what about you? Who do you say I am?"*

The disciples looked at each other uncomfortably, trying to guess the tenure of Jesus' question. But Simon Peter spoke up and answered, *"You are the Christ, the Son of the Living God."* Peter had a new revelation of who Christ really was and where Jesus had come from. Peter had been given a first hand revelation of the identity of Jesus. The Father had so graciously revealed this to Peter who was a simple fisherman.

Suddenly a new realm of understanding came upon Simon Peter, as if his entire life had been leading up to this crucial declaration. Jesus immediately announced that Peter was blessed for having been given this insight from the Father. No longer would he be Simon "the unsteady"; from now on he would be known as Peter "the Rock." He would possess greater authority and would become a cornerstone of the future church. Peter had found himself.

What Happened?

Why would such an apparently simple conclusion be so paramount? Jesus had told the disciples all along that He was the Son of God. What so different about Peter's declaration?

The difference was that Peter gained an understanding of his own identity *because he understood by faith the iden-*

tity of Jesus! To put it another way, until Peter understood
who Jesus was, he could not begin to understand himself.
As Christians, we must come to the point that we know Jesus
in order to understand our freedom in Him. Our identity—
who we are—must be anchored in the reality of who He is:

He is the Rock...therefore we are unshakable.
He is the Almighty...therefore we are confident.
He is Holy...therefore we are sanctified in Him.
He is the Savior...therefore we have eternal life.
He is the Provider...therefore we have provision.
He is Love...therefore we have security.

Because Jesus is the great "I Am"—the ultimate reality—we can become identified with the power of His resurrection and truly understand who we are. Read Paul's words
from Philippians 2:1-2:

"Therefore if there is any consolation in Christ, if
any comfort of love, if any fellowship of the Spirit, if
any affection and mercy, fulfill my joy by being like-
minded, having the same love, being of one accord,
of one mind."

Paul's joy can only be made complete if Christians are
one with each other and with Christ—completely identified
with the Savior. Why would this complete the apostle's joy?
Because Paul understood that the only way Christians can
have true freedom and spiritual ability is by completely surrendering to the cause of Christ and identifying ourselves
with Him. We must consistently, on a daily basis, strive to
have our lives conform into the image of Christ.
Someone once said: "Understanding your identity in
Christ is absolutely essential to your success at living the
victorious Christian life."[1] The old song says, "There is power

in the blood of the Lamb." There is also power in identifying ourselves with Christ and discovering who we are in Him!

> **Power to Change!**
> **Power to Deliver!**
> **Power to Pray!**
> **Power to Heal!**
> **Power to Witness!**
> **Power to Live!**

Finding Ourselves in Jesus

What does it mean to identify with Jesus? It means that we know who we are based upon our relationship with Christ, and that we now believe that everything the Bible says is possible can be accomplished in our life as a result of that identification. We can't truly know ourselves without knowing our Creator. Christians who are accomplishing great things for God have their identity securely in Jesus. They know God, therefore they know God is at work in them. Remember Daniel's great words: "...*the people who know their God will display strength and take action*" Daniel 11:32 (NAS).

I was talking to a friend of mine, Tim Storey. At the time I was just getting back with the Lord and being discipled in a class taught by this great man of God. I had been struggling with who I was, and my self-esteem. Then Tim told me something that totally revolutionized my life. He said, "Benny, God's opinion of you makes man's opinion irrelevant—find out what God says about you!" That statement was the phrase God used to catapult me out of a low level of living into the high living of the Spirit of God. I went on a personal journey to find out who I was in Jesus. If we are going to set the pace for this world we must know who we are in Christ.

Ephesian Interlude

Let's take a journey to Ephesus and see a tremendous illustration of the importance of knowing who we are. But first, a little historical background...

Ephesus was an important commercial and cultural center in the ancient world. It had been colonized originally by the Greeks, and then was ruled by the Persians, the Macedonians and finally by Paul's time, the Romans. The population during the ministry of Paul was around 300,000 citizens and slaves. The Ephesians were as religious as they were industrious, and focused mainly on the goddess Diana, whose great temple, with 127 columns reaching a height of 197 feet, was one of the Seven Wonders of the Ancient World.

Apart from the recognized religions of the day which were practiced within Ephesus, a large number of occult groups thrived within the city. Fortune tellers, diviners, magicians and other occult opportunists preyed upon the people. The silversmiths were making a killing selling little images of the goddess Diana. It is little wonder that the letter from Paul to the Ephesian church deals largely with spiritual warfare—the city was rampant with demonic activity!

When Paul arrived in Ephesus during his second missionary journey the Lord worked marvelous miracles through him. These people needed convincing! Another holy man with a teaching just wasn't going to cut it without some sort of powerful demonstration. Paul was just one of hundreds of religious fanatics unless he could pull off something convincing and extraordinary . That's just what God did!

"Now God worked unusual miracles by the hands of Paul, so that even handkerchiefs or aprons were brought from his body to the sick, and the diseases left them and the evil spirits went out of them.

Then some of the itinerant Jewish exorcists took it upon themselves to call the name of the Lord Jesus over those who had evil spirits, saying, 'We exorcise you by the Jesus who Paul preaches.'

Also, there were seven sons of Sceva, a Jewish chief priest, who did so.

And the evil spirit answered and said, 'Jesus I know, and Paul I know; but who are you?'

Then the man in whom the evil spirit was leaped on them, overpowered them, and prevailed against them, so that they fled out of that house naked and wounded.

This became known both to all Jews and Greeks dwelling in Ephesus; and fear fell upon them all, and the name of the Lord Jesus was magnified.

And many who had believed came confessing and telling their deeds.

Also, many of those who had practiced magic brought their books together and burned them in the sight of all. And they counted up the value of them, and it totaled fifty thousand pieces of silver.

So the word of the Lord grew mightily and prevailed" Acts 19:11-20.

God's Power Unleashed

Paul plainly knew his God. He knew that there was nothing in and of himself which would work any miracle or heal even the smallest wound. But he also realized that God desired to demonstrate His authority within a city beset by demonic strongholds. At times throughout the Bible, God uses His power in order to declare to the world His existence and supremacy, thus serving notice on creation that the Creator is, in fact, alive and well. When God brought judgment upon Egypt it was not only to force Pharaoh into

letting the Israelites go free, but also to humble the Egyptian deities represented by the particular plagues.
Demonic manifestations are not a thing of the past, either. Missionaries report that the Third World countries are swarming with demonic activity. There are several reasons for this, but primarily it is because the people in these cultures are open to the demonic. A voodoo witch doctor might be right at home in downtown Haiti, but he would look a little out of place in downtown Seattle, Washington. (Of course there are certain parts of this country where he might look right at home!) The point is that demonic powers are resident everywhere, but they are particularly noticeable in underdeveloped regions because the people living there are more open to such activity.

Don't take too much comfort in this. Just because America is not given to such manifestations because of our cosmopolitan, rational outlook does not mean that demonic strongholds are not trying to bring us down. Just a brief look at a daily newspaper, or a cruise through television channels late at night will prove that there is something devilish afoot in our country. Mom and apple pie have been replaced by psychic hotlines and cyber porn. Unless someone is willing to set the pace for this generation, America has little prospects for the future. Are you willing?

God's Ability + Paul's Availability = Revival

The passage from Acts 19:11 makes it clear that Paul was **not** the miracle worker; the honor and glory went to God. However, God often chooses to work through people in order to execute His will. In Ephesus, Paul was the man of the hour who was available and willing. He was a *pacesetter* that ended up authoring most of the New Testament.

Remember that God is always looking for people to stand in the gap so that His power can move among people. Who is He using in your community? Could it perhaps be you?

We must be careful not to judge who God will or will not use. Our tendency is to look toward outer ability and physical attractiveness as to whether or not a person has the goods. God looks at the heart of an individual—the inner person—regardless of their humanity. David's brothers found this out in a very humbling way when each of them was turned down by Samuel as God's chosen, only to witness the anointing of their little, tag-along brother, David, as king. God will often call the most unlikely people to do extraordinary tasks.

God Wants You!

During the Second World War there was a very famous recruiting poster which pictured Uncle Sam pointing at the reader with the words emblazoned underneath: "I Want You!" I believe God is saying the same thing to Christians all over the world:

I Want You...
...to be a person willing to set the pace for this world,
...to stand up for what is right,
...to set trends and not follow them,
...to honor God with your life,
...to pay the price to see God's power touch a hurting generation.

God wants Christians to be His instrument to execute judgment on the powers of darkness in their world, just as Paul did at Ephesus. He is looking for individuals regardless of looks, race, social status, popularity, and all the rest, into whom He can pour His Spirit and power and see darkness give way to light. Never turn down an opportunity to serve God...and never doubt your ability to do what He has called you to perform. God will work the miracles...but you need to know who you are in Christ in order for Him to do so.

It's Not What You Know...But Who You Know

Knowledge opens many doors...but relationship gets you invited inside. So it is with ministry. Greatness in ministry begins with relationship to God. Why? Because the closer you grow to God, the more you will understand yourself and your limitations; therefore, the more you will depend upon God to accomplish His will through you. This is the hard lesson those seven unfortunate Jews learned when they tried to oppose a demon with only a cognitive experience with Jesus. They knew about Jesus—but they didn't *know* Jesus.

According to the reading in Acts, there were groups of Jews who were in the deliverance ministry about the same time Paul was preaching in Ephesus. These well-intentioned men went around looking for demonized people in order to exorcise the evil spirit. Apparently they had a measure of success, though most likely their ability to cast out demons was either unreal or temporary at best, since they did not invoke the name of Jesus. Instead they used a form of divination to drive out the demons—attempting finally to use Jesus' name like an incantation rather than in faith.

As they had probably witnessed Paul's ministry and had seen for themselves that demons responded to the name of Jesus, they decided that they would also begin to drive out demons in this name. Therein lay the mistake which cost them a beating. The Jews attempted to use the name of Jesus without any significant relationship *to* Jesus. The result was a false confidence upon the part of the Jews and utter contempt on the part of the evil spirit. Let me illustrate.

If I go to the Microsoft Corporation headquarters and tell the receptionist on the executive floor that I want to look around because I think that Bill Gates is a great guy and a wonderful entrepreneur, I'll have security on me before I even get to say the word "entrepreneur." However, if I am friends with Bill Gates and I tell that same secretary that I know Bill Gates personally, I will be allowed greater access to the office. It's not what I know, but who I know which will make the difference of whether or not I gain access.

The Jews had seen Paul use the name of Jesus with great success. The difference was that they only knew about Jesus—Paul knew Jesus. Paul had relationship with Christ which gave him the access and authority to cast out demons and perform miracles. These seven Jews, called the sons of Sceva, (who was the chief priest of the Jews in Ephesus) grew up in a religious world. They were familiar with Jewish tradition and ritual. They were like kids who grow up in church but miss out on the real thing even when it is all around them. Just because their father was a high priest did not make them better Jews, anymore than a parent's relationship with Christ will make their children Christians. Each of us is responsible for a first-hand encounter with Jesus—a first-hand revelation which we receive directly from God.

"In the Name of Jesus Whom Paul Preaches..."

The seven Jews unwittingly found themselves in trouble because they tried to encounter first-hand darkness with second-hand light. In other words, their knowledge of Jesus was only hearsay—something they never personally experienced. If you watched any of the O.J. Simpson trial, you might recall that certain testimonies by witnesses were inadmissible because they were only hearsay; that is, they were words never heard directly spoken by the defendant but words the defendant had supposedly said to someone else who then relayed the information to the witness. It was ruled inadmissible because the witness never personally heard the defendant say these things.

The seven brothers were trying to cast out a demon by hearsay—second-hand revelation. What they needed to knock the spirit out was first-hand revelation. First hand revelation gives us:

- **Supernatural ability,**
- **Supernatural faith,**
- **Supernatural confidence,**
- **Supernatural wisdom.**

Without first-hand revelation, which comes from personal relationship with God, we don't stand a chance. The demon world shudders at the thought of Jesus Christ and those who know Him. But they will always send a person packing who claims knowledge of Jesus without knowing Him relationally. Remember that it is not what you know, but Who you know that really counts. The kingdom of God is built on relationship with God, which comes through the Word and prayer. These two aspects of the Christian life are the keys to knowing God and how He works.

"Jesus I Know, Paul I Have Heard About... But Who Are you?"

On the particular day when these vagabond Jews decided to invoke the name of Jesus they got more than they bargained for. At some point we will have an encounter with darkness—the day is appointed. The question is, do you know Jesus? They came across a demon-possessed man and used the name of Jesus in a second-hand manner: "In the name of Jesus who Paul preaches...".

The demon's answer is interesting. He declares truth and tells the men, "Jesus I know, and Paul I have heard about, but who are you?"

"Jesus I know..."

The Greek text uses two different words for "to know" in this passage. The demon says, "Jesus I know." In the Greek the word know is "ginosko" indicating intimate knowledge and awareness of something by prior experience or recognition. The demon is in effect saying I am totally aware of who Jesus is because I have known him before this occasion. This demon might have encountered Jesus personally. The demon remembered that Jesus destroyed all demonic power through the cross. Jesus made an open show of them all and now, at the name of Jesus, demon forces must bow.

"...and I know about Paul..."

The word used for "knowing Paul" in this verse is in the Greek "epistamai" which indicates an understanding. The demon understands Paul's authority and therefore respects him, whether or not he has actually encountered Paul face to face. It's as if Paul's reputation has preceded him in the spirit realm and demons are aware that this guy is big trouble. Oh, how I want to have such a reputation in the corridors of hell! I want the enemy to know that I have an intimate relationship with Jesus and I know the authority I have in Jesus. The world around us and the spirit realm are looking for Pacesetters to take a stand and know who we are in Christ.

"...but who are you?"

These seven guys trying to cast him out—who in the world are they? This is the trick and message of Satan to the world today—*Who are you?* This is the question that he is posing to all Christians in an attempt to rattle their faith. As believers in Jesus, we need to continually affirm our position in Christ. We must realize who we are by realizing who Christ is. Jesus promised that the world would only grow more and more wicked, particularly as the last days approached. Our authority and position in Christ must be ever increasing if we are to be the pacesetters this world needs. Peter and James warn us in their epistles of our need to be armed and dangerous:

"Be sober, be vigilant; because your adversary the devil walks about like a roaring lion, seeking whom he may devour. Resist him, steadfast in the faith, knowing that the same sufferings are experienced by your brotherhood in the world" I Peter 5:8-9.

"Therefore submit to God. Resist the devil and he will flee from you. Draw near to God and He will draw near to you. Cleanse your hands, you sinners; and purify your hearts you double-minded" James 4:7-8.

Notice that both of these men admonish believers to recognize that the enemy is very real, but that he can be handled by first-hand revelation and relationship to God. We can only resist the enemy if the Spirit of God lives inside of us, and that can only happen if we have a sincere relationship with Jesus.

"He Gave Them Such a Beating..."

The result of fighting a battle without the proper equipment was both humorous and tragic. The men were sat upon by the demon-possessed man who ran them out of the house naked and bleeding—and no doubt right out of the deliverance ministry! It's kind of like the old joke that says they brought a knife to a gunfight. They were beaten before the encounter even started because the demon had no respect for these Jews.

I once saw a man at a golf course step out of his cart and approach the first tee. He looked immaculate—expensive set of clubs, sharp-looking clothes, confidence all over his face. He looked every inch the pro...until he tried to play golf. He was simply not very good. He might have looked the part, but he should have just hung around the clubhouse where he was a convincing golfer instead of demonstrating his true abilities by actually attempting to play.

This is how many Christians operate—a religious manner which masquerades emptiness. I love this quote by noted preacher Vance Havner:

> *"We are a generation of cheap Christians going to heaven as inexpensively as possible; religious hobos and spiritual deadbeats living on milk instead of meat, crusts of bread instead of manna, as though we were on a cut-rate excursion."*[2]

The Bible says that in the last days people will have a form of godliness but will deny its power. But people want to be convinced! **The world is looking for the real thing! People are without hope and want to see true power, just as Paul convinced the Ephesians of God's authority!**

The World Is Dying to Be
Convinced of Something Real

The result of Paul's ministry in Ephesus and the encounter with the demon-possessed man by the sons of Sceva were dramatic. They suddenly recognized that the spiritual world was in a state of war and were seized with fear. They were afraid and began to revere the name of Jesus. Like the Jews who had been beaten, the Ephesians began to realize that there was indeed something special about the name of Jesus and they wanted to know more about Him. Jesus was the only real protection they could have against demons and they wanted that assurance.

Not only were the people fearing God, but the word of the Lord was held in high esteem, especially the name of Jesus. They realized that there is power in the name of Jesus when it is applied in faith from a first-hand revelation. Again, having a first-hand revelation is knowing God for yourself. God has become personal and intimate to you, not only to your parents, pastors or peers. Having a first-revelation will move you into action that will bring success.

I remember when I was ministering one time in a local church in Apple Valley, California. I had just finished preaching a message on the power of the name of Jesus. I made an altar call and a young lady came forward. I laid my hands on her and prayed that Jesus would touch her. Just then the young lady fell to the floor and began moving around like she was having convulsions. She proceeded to talk in a male voice and had unusual strength. The girl was demonized and had to be delivered. I can remember praying for her and the demon saying to me, "I am not coming out and you cannot make me!" Well, I was taken back and to be quite honest, I was scared. I stepped back having fear running through my body when all of a sudden the Holy Spirit filled me with faith. The Lord spoke to my heart and said that the demon was not defying me but the Lord God Himself. At that moment I received a first hand revelation that the demon could not defy God because Jesus had already defeated all demon power at the cross. The demon had to go because it was not my power but God's power flowing through me. With this added faith, and first-hand revelation, I saw God bring a mighty deliverance to the young lady.

Revival Breaks Out

Someone once said that you know it's revival when the Christians begin repenting! So it was at Ephesus as believers began to openly confess their sins and repent before God. They wanted to make sure that there was no open door for the enemy to access—no root of bitterness, no filthy habit, nothing to which a demonic stronghold could attach itself.

They also did something remarkable: they brought all their occult artifacts, in this case magic scrolls, and burned them as a demonstration of their true change of heart. Many times I have had young people bring everything from CD's, drugs, magazines, weapons to cigarettes that we burned in a huge fire to illustrate to the world and the devil that deliverance had come to their lives.

The result of all these events was that the Word of God spread widely and the power of God intensified. All because a man named Paul knew who he was in Christ and allowed God to use him in an extraordinary way. How about you? Are you receiving first-hand revelation from God, or are you trying to know Him from a distance? God's challenge to those who want to do great exploits for Him is to know Him, not know about Him. Pacesetters for this generation know who they are, because they know God.

---

1. Neil T. Anderson and Dave Park, Stomping Out the Darkness, (Ventura: Regal Books, 1993), p. 39.
2. Bob & Michael Benson, Disciplines for the Inner Life, (Waco: Word Books, 1985), p. 4.
3. Vance Havner, The Vance Havner Quote Book, Compiled by Dennis J. Hester, (Grand Rapids: Baker Book House, 1986) p. 36.

Chapter Three

Setting the Pace By Running the Race

"It is not the critic who counts; not the man who points out how the strong man stumbled, or where the doer of deeds could have done better. The credit belongs to the man who is actually in the arena; whose face is marred by dust and sweat and blood; who strives valiantly; who errs and comes short again and again; who know the great enthusiasms, the great devotions and spends himself in a worthy cause; who at the best knows in the end the triumph of high achievement; and who at the worst, if he fails, at least fails while daring greatly; so that his place shall never be with those cold and timid souls who know neither victory nor defeat."[1]

Theodore Roosevelt

Did you know you are in a race? Either willingly or unwillingly, knowingly or completely oblivious; you are in a race. And so is everyone else. If you don't believe me just take a look outside your office window, or in your school hallways between classes, or even in your church on a busy Sunday morning. What you'll see is people trying to get somewhere in various states of mind, from the contented and happy to the frustrated and angry. The race is on!

Our society is in a race against itself and nobody is winning. Everyone is trying to achieve some measure of satisfaction but the goal remains illusive. America has lost it's direction and is expending more and more energy trying to grasp some sort of fulfillment: better bodies, better minds, better love-lives, better everything. The end result is only better ulcers and better frustration! In an attempt to become better we frequently end up bitter.

In their book, *We Are Driven*, Doctors Robert Hemfelt, Frank Minrith and Paul Meier write, "We live in a culture that is constantly chasing the false gods of materialism and achievement. It's no surprise that many people are facing depression, chronic fatigue syndrome and burnout."[1] The book goes on to report that we have become a nation driven by the need to succeed and achieve at any cost, running the race toward a mirage of happiness.

Which Way Now?

In the Sermon on the Mount, Jesus challenged the people to be careful which path in life they chose:

> *"Enter by the narrow gate; for wide is the gate and broad is the way that leads to destruction, and there are many who go in by it. Because narrow is the gate and difficult is the way which leads to life, and there are few who find it"* Matthew 7:13-14.

Though there seems to be many choices offered to us, there are really only two which matter: the path of eternal life or the path of eternal death. God is challenging us to choose life through a first-hand revelation relationship with His Son, Jesus Christ. As Pacesetters, we must blaze a trail for others to follow, leading to everlasting life with the Father. We must, ourselves, be willing to run the race and endure hardship for the cause of Christ.

Running to Win

In his letter to the Corinthian church, Paul admonished the Christians to live completely unto the Lord Jesus. He instructed them in many areas, including marriage, disciplining a fellow believer, taking communion, spiritual gifts and other important doctrinal issues. The main problem Paul was facing with the Corinthians was that they came out of a totally hedonistic and pagan background which filtered through their Christian witness. They were still Christians but they were "carnally minded" according to Paul. The apostle came up with a great metaphor to illustrate the idea of pursuing Christ with all fervency.

Corinth was among the leading cities of Greece. Apart from a rich commerce and culture, the Corinthians hosted the Olympic games from time to time. As a result, the citizens were very sports-minded and competitive. Paul uses an illustration from the world of sports to effectively make his point:

> "Do you not know that those who run in a race all run, but one receives the prize? Run in such a way that you may obtain it.
> And everyone who competes for the prize is temperate in all things. Now they do it to obtain a perishable crown, but we for an imperishable crown.

Therefore I run thus: not with uncertainty. Thus I fight: not as one who beats the air.
But I discipline my body and bring it into subjection, lest, when I have preached to others, I myself should become disqualified" I Corinthians 9:24-27.

Notice that Paul says that "all run" in the race—everyone of us is entered as a participant—but there can be only one winner in a competition. I once was working a crossword puzzle in a newspaper. I was looking for a five-letter word, and the clue given was "second-place." The word turned out to be "loser." Pretty harsh, but accurate. Second-place is nice, but the blue ribbon is reserved for whoever comes in first.

God has geared us to be motivated by certain incentives and benefits. If something is worthwhile to us, we will strive to attain that particular goal. The greatest prize available to all of us is eternal life. God has made a way for us to attain life everlasting by simply receiving salvation by faith. It is then our responsibility to run the race of life in an appropriate manner demonstrating that we are running the race for Christ. Remember that Jesus made it clear that we must bear fruit, thus showing we are truly His disciples and are in the race of life. The goal is always ahead of us and we must run to win!

How Do We Run?

In his autobiography, former Dallas Cowboys coach, Tom Landry, writes, "The primary challenge of coaching in the National Football League can be boiled down to a one-sentence job description: **To get people to do what they don't want to do in order to achieve what they want to achieve.**"[2] Coach Landry makes the point that in order to be a winner, one must adhere to certain principles and disciplines, while running a hard-fought race. He believes the apostle Paul serves as a prime illustration of running the race well:

"The apostle Paul is one of my favorite biblical characters because he was such a competitor. He was stoned, shipwrecked, imprisoned, and still he wouldn't quit...Paul understood what it took to be a champion and a successful leader. He realized that the quality of a man's life was in direct proportion to his commitment to excellence."[3]

As *Pacesetters*, we must come to the place where we will do whatever it takes, even the things which we don't want to do, in order to be winners for the kingdom of God. Like Paul and Coach Landry, we must develop a commitment to excellence which propels us toward the finish line, whatever the odds.

Formula for the Race

We just read Tom Landry's formula for success based upon a commitment to excellence and helping people push to the limit even when they don't want to be pushed. Now let's examine Paul's formula for running a race.

1. We must focus on heaven itself as our finish line.

We must earnestly pursue the goal of heaven. It must consume our passion and drive us to serve God with greater and greater energy. We have to view our journey on earth as a race which we have determined to win, even at tremendous personal cost. Paul was willing to give up everything for the sake of winning the race. In his letter to the Philippians he wrote:

"But what things were gain to me, these I have counted loss for Christ.

Yet indeed I count all things loss for the excellence of the knowledge of Christ Jesus my Lord, for whom I have suffered the loss of all things, and count them as rubbish that I may gain Christ.

Not that I have already attained, or am already perfected; but I press on, that I may lay hold of that for which Christ Jesus has already laid hold of me.

Brethren, I do not count myself to have apprehended; but one thing I do, forgetting those things which are behind and reaching forward to those things which are ahead,

I press toward the goal for the prize of the upward call of God in Christ Jesus" Philippians 3:7-8, 12-14.

Paul had come to a point in his life where nothing else mattered except running the race with excellence. All his past achievements, successes, dreams and knowledge meant zero compared to knowing Jesus Christ as Lord. We also need to come to a place where we are willing to crucify everything else in order to run a good race; to forget the past and look toward our heavenly goal.

2. We must run with endurance.

Paul told us that only one person can win a race; therefore, we should compete as a champion. The book of Hebrews encourages us to compete vigorously because there is more at stake than a personal victory:

"Therefore we also, since we are surrounded by so great a cloud of witnesses, let us lay aside every weight, and the sin which so easily ensnares us, and let us run with endurance the race that is set before

us, looking unto Jesus, the author and finisher of our faith, who for the joy that was et before Him endured the cross, depising the sham, and has set down at the right hand of the throne of God.

For consider Him who endured such hostility from sinners against Himself, lest you become weary and discouraged in your souls." Hebrews 12:1-2.

We are encouraged to look at the suffering of Jesus as our example of endurance. Jesus could have come off the cross at any moment, but because the greater purpose of His ministry necessitated His death, He went through the pain and shame of the cross. What motivated and encouraged Him to continue on in the struggle? The joy of seeing you and me and every other believer who has called upon the name of the Lord *since* His death and resurrection! That joy became the strength which carried Him through. What about Christians today? What motivates us to carry on through to the finish? The same joy!

We recognize what a joy it is when we are living a great testimony to God and running a good race and bringing people to heaven in our wake. Christians should have a burning desire to not only see Jesus personally one day, but to present to Him as many saved people as possible. That is why the victory is not just a personal triumph. Talk about joy!

3. We must be willing to enter into strict training.

Here it comes...the "D" word...discipline. Paul's Olympic example and Landry's football career all point to the same principle; a winner builds discipline into his or her life. Nobody ever said that rules, regulations, and training were easy or fun all of the time. But they are necessary. The famous concert pianist, Vladmir Horowitz, once remarked about practicing the piano each day for several hours: "If I go a day without practice, I can tell the difference. If I go two days without practice, my wife can tell the difference. And if I go three days without practice, everybody can tell the difference!"

As the writer in Hebrews states, we must lay aside the things which will entangle or distract us and follow the course with focus and resolve—and we must play by the rules. Paul tells his young disciple, Timothy:

> *"If anyone competes in athletics, he is not crowned unless he competes according to the rules"* II Timothy 2:5.

Jesus declares a similar truth in John 10:

> *"Most assuredly I say to you, he who does not enter the sheepfold by the door, but climbs up some other way, the same is a thief and a robber"* John 10:1.

Jesus warned his disciples that there would come a time when people who were only believers in appearance would find their way into the sheepfold. These are people who run a race by another set of rules, playing the religious game so well they even fool themselves. Though they believe they are safely inside, they are in for a tragic awakening one day when Jesus will plainly tell them, *"Depart from Me, I never knew you."* Remember this important principle: Winning is important, but only if we win according to God's faith principles. If we live by God's principles, then God will cause us to prosper so that we can help others live the life of a Pacesetter.

I remember several years ago when the Lord prompted me to discipline myself and spend my Friday and Satruday nights seeking Him. So every Friday I was seeking the Lord from nine to twelve midnight in the chapel at First Family

Church in Whittier, California. It started out to be discipline but later turned into a delight. Oh, the intimacy that I experienced those early years I spent seeking the Lord! I know thatI was entering into strict training.

4. We must run with absolute confidence in victory.
In his example, Paul says that we must run with purpose, not like a man boxing the air with his fists. We can only find direction from our relationship to God through His Word and prayer. Paul was a man with a purpose and a destination; he was guided, empowered and encouraged by the Lord. If we know we are going to win and if we run with the assurance of Christ's victory, then the race will always be competitive and well-run.

Toward the end of his life, Paul was able to reflect on a job well done. Just as Jesus was able to say, *"It is finished"* before he died, so Paul was able to write with confidence to Timothy:

> *"I have fought the good fight, I have finished the race, I have kept the faith.*
> *Finally, there is laid up for me the crown of righteousness, which the Lord, the righteous Judge, will give to me on that Day, and not to me only but to all who have loved His appearing"* II Timothy 4:7-8.

What a testimony! Paul's days were numbered; he would soon face the executioner's ax by order of Nero. Yet his perspective to the very end was ever heavenward. If we are going to set the pace for our friends and family, we must demonstrate that same resolve to finish, and to finish well. The great writer, Washington Irving, wrote: "Little minds are subdued by misfortunes; but great minds rise above them." Since we possess the mind of Christ, we can rise above anything.

5. We must keep our bodies under discipline.
I mentioned discipline in connection with training and rules, but we must also bring our bodies under strict dominance as well. If I allow my own passions and desires to be in charge, I will never persevere in the race. Why? Because the Bible says that the spirit and the flesh are at war with one another, each seeking to dominate the other. We must allow the Spirit of God to have absolute control of our lives or else the flesh will tend to dominate. Paul asked the Galatians:

"Are you so foolish? Having begun in the spirit are you now being made perfect by the flesh?" Galatians 3:3.

We can't begin the race strong spiritually and then try to complete the remainder of the contest in the natural or physical realm. From the start to the finish we must be operating in the spiritual or we will never finish the race. But what does Paul mean by being "in the spirit"? Let's see what he says in the letter to the Romans:

"But you are not in the flesh but in the Spirit, if indeed the Spirit of God dwells in you. Now if anyone does not have the Spirit of Christ he is not His.
And if Christ is in you, the body is dead because of sin, but the Spirit is life because of righteousness.
But if the Spirit of Him who raised Jesus from the dead dwells in you, He who raised Christ from the dead will also give life to your mortal bodies through His Spirit who dwells in you.
Therefore, brethren, we are debtors—not to the flesh, to live according to the flesh.
For if you live according to the flesh you will die; but if by the Spirit you put to death the deeds of the body, you will live.

For as many as are led by the Spirit of God, these are the sons of God" Romans 8:9-14.

"I beseech you therefore, brethren, by the mercies of God, that you present your bodies a living sacrifice, holy, acceptable to God, which is your reasonable service.

And do not be conformed to this world, but be transformed by the renewing of your mind, that you may prove what is the good and acceptable and perfect will of God" Romans 12:1-2.

Living in the Spirit is a matter of our recognizing that there is a contest between the flesh and the spirit, and then overcoming our flesh by faith in the power of the Spirit. The work of the Cross has dealt a mortal blow to the flesh; it is up to us to appropriate the faith necessary to be overcomers.

We are also challenged not to compromise and go along with the standards of the world, but to live according to standards set forth in God's Word.

Christians must set the pace, not follow the trends!

How do we renew our minds? By studying the Word of God which produces faith and wisdom; by meditating on the goodness of God; by prayer; by worship; by fellowship with other believers. A renewed mind allows God to show us His will, and therefore the course our race should follow. To run a good race we must have a renewed mind which will allow us to understand and confidently appropriate God's will and direction for our lives.

6. We must rely upon the coach and gain strength from Him.

During the dark days of World War II, England alone stood to challenge the might of Nazi Germany. Flushed with victory on the Continent, Germany was poised to force Britain to her knees. To the world it only seemed a matter of time before England, like France before her, would go down in defeat. But a remarkable thing happened. A pudgy, cigar-smoking, little man with a speech impediment came to power; his name was Winston Churchill. He became a *pacesetter* that changed the world.

He began to extol the virtues of freedom and rallied the people to dig in for the fight; he told the people that they must never contemplate surrender; he set the nation on a crusade to rid the world of Nazism. The people responded as if they were awakened from a trance and a new fighting spirit was born. At one point immediately after the fall of France, the French government in exile pleaded with Churchill to send planes and troops to save France. Churchill remarked that he had none to send. The French generals told him that Hitler was going to "ring England's neck like a chicken." A few months later when the tide of battle was more favorable for the British, Churchill recounted the story to the Canadian parliament adding: "Some chicken...some neck!"

We have in the Lord the greatest leadership possible. He is a consummate general, a brilliant tactician, and an ingenious strategist. Not only that, He is a player-coach! He not only sends us out onto the field, He accompanies us the entire game. We can trust the leadership of our Lord. Look at what the psalmist said about God going before us:

> *"For by You I can run against a troop, by my God I can leap over a wall, As for God, His way is perfect; the word of the Lord is proven; He is a shield to all who trust in Him"* Psalm 18:29-30.

Not only does God call us to run the race with endurance, but He promises to blaze the trail ahead of us! God is a magnificent leader who will never leave us to the enemy's pleasure. He is able to run through any adversity and conquer any obstacle. Thank God we are fighting with Him and not against Him! He is our Pacesetter so that we can set the pace for others.

7. We must run with the right people.
Remember what Jesus said about the sheepfold? There will be some who are legitimate, and some who are not. We can expect that as we run the race we will come in contact with some believers who are sincerely fighting the good fight, and some who only appear to be in the conflict. It is important that we partner with the right people while fighting the good fight. Paul warned about this in his letter to the Philippians:

> *"Brethren, join in following my example, and note those who so walk, as you have us for a pattern.*
> *For many walk, of whom I have told you often, and now tell you even weeping, that they are the enemies of the cross of Christ"* Philippians 3:17-18.

Like a good leader who is confident in his abilities, Paul instructs the believers at Philippi to follow his pattern, and reminds them that some who appeared to be in the faith have turned traitor. The lesson is clear: Be careful who you follow and with whom you run! I have a best friend named Iann Schonken, who I had the priviledge of meeting during my college days at S.C.C. He is a man who is like-minded and runs with the same passion and zeal for the Lord. I had the opportunity to be room mates with him for a whole year. It was during this year that I truly saw that this was a man who really loved the Lord. He encouraged and propelled me to higher heights in God. I knew that God had given me a dear brother with whom I could run and depend upon. Iann and I continue to run together as we encourage each other to be all that God has called us to be.

We are also commanded not to partner with someone who is not like-minded in the things of God. Paul calls the relationship between a believer and a non-believer an unequal yoking; that is, a relationship which is out of balance and harmful.

"Do not be unequally yoked together with unbelievers. For what fellowship has righteousness with lawlessness? And what communion has light with darkness?" II Corinthians 6:14.

Jesus taught us the same principle when He said that a little bit of yeast in a lump of dough will eventually effect all of the dough. We cannot run a good race if we are weighed down in our relationships with the world. We are to be salt and light to the world. Our fellowship must be limited to what the Lord allows as needful for the unsaved for the purposes of redemption and other ministry. Are you running for the prize—or are you just running? Those who would be Pacesetters must not only be running for the prize, but doing so with perseverance and purity as an example for those who might follow. Let us join Paul and fight the good fight to the very end.

---

1. Andy Andrews, Storms of Perfection, Nashville: Lightning Crown Publishers, 1992, p. 43.
2. Dr. Robert Hemfelt, Dr. Frank Minrith, Dr. Paul Meier, We Are Driven, (Nashville: Thomas Nelson Publishers, 1991).
3. Tom Landry, Tom Landry: An Autobiography, (Grand Rapids: Zondervan Publishing House, 1990), p. 269.
4. Ibid, p. 288.

Chapter Four

The Bigger They Are...

"We are inclined to think God chooses "big names" to do important jobs. So we showcase celebrities who are Christians: baseball stars, politicians, beauty queens, millionaires. But Paul disagreed. He knew that our heavenly Father uses little people. His key point: It's our weakness God wants, more than our strength; our accessibility, more than our ability." [1]

From <u>Christian Excellence</u> by Jon Johnston

In the previous chapter I illustrated the importance of running the race of life. We learned that not only is everyone in the race, but we are called to run as winners. We noted some key components to running a good race:

1. We must focus on heaven itself as our finish line.
2. We must run with endurance.
3. We must be willing to enter into strict training.
4. We must run with absolute confidence in victory.
5. We must keep our bodies under discipline.
6. We must rely on our coach and gain strength from Him.
7. We must run with like-minded people.

Why is winning so important? Because God is calling us to victory in Christ! I believe that Christians have taken it on the chin long enough and it is time to rise up and take a stand for righteousness in this country. God is not satisfied with status quo churches who do little from Sunday to Sunday except gather together, sing a few songs, and have pie and coffee afterwards.

God is looking to pour His Spirit into a radical people who will manifest His supernatural powers and execute vengeance upon the powers of darkness. He is desiring a church who is an example of holiness and purity in a world drunk on wickedness and depravity. He is looking for a generation of believers who are not afraid to stand up and be counted among those who believe in and call upon the Lord Jesus Christ; who are devoted to their families; who earn an honest day's labor; who serve in their churches; who love their country. I believe that God is looking for people whom I call Pacesetters.

What Is a Pacesetter?

A Pacesetter is a person or a group of people who serve as an example or model for godly living that others may follow. The motto which Pacesetters follow is simple, but significant:

Setting the Standard, Not Following the Trend!

A Pacesetter doesn't follow the patterns of the world, feels no need to compromise just because "everyone else is," and does not imitate the people around them just to fit in. A Pacesetter acts on the truth of God's Word regardless of what others might think, in order to faithfully bring reconciliation and deliverance to our lost world.

The Bible is full of Pacesetters, men and women who laid it all on the line in order to follow God's will for their lives. Some that come to mind readily include:

Noah—who was called upon to build an enormous boat because of a rainy forecast, even though it had never rained before that time.

Abraham—a man who left the security of country and family to embark upon an unknown destiny in a far-off place called Canaan.

Moses—who gave up the splendors of Egypt to lead an unruly nation to a promised land.

Esther— a woman who laid it all on the line by approaching the king on behalf of her people, even though she risked her life in doing so.

There are so many other great examples of Pacesetters in the Word of God. But in this chapter we'll focus on a man who set the pace for his nation and changed forever the course of human history: David.

Probably one of the most revered and recognized biblical characters apart from Jesus Christ Himself, is David. The story of the shepherd-boy-becoming-king is compelling as a rags-to-riches story of a "nobody" making good. We love David because his sincere faith, his heroic encounter with Goliath, his deep love for God, his godliness and his human flaws. All of these make David a desirable person to emulate and an encouragement to all that God can use whoever is available and willing.

The story of David begins in the book of First Samuel during one of the many wars Israel waged against their antagonistic neighbors to the south, the Philistines. As we look upon the battlelines which have been drawn on either side of the valley of Elah, we see two different attitudes prevailing within the camps.

> *"Now the Philistines gathered their armies together to battle, and were gathered at Sochoh, which belongs to Judah; they encamped between Sochoh and Azekah, in Ephes Dammin.*
>
> *And Saul and the men of Israel were gathered together, and they encamped in the Valley of Elah, and drew up in battle array against the Philistines.*
>
> *The Philistines stood on a mountain on one side, and Israel stood on a mountain on the other side, with a valley between them"* I Samuel 17:1-3.

Some striking observations can be made at once in this text. Notice first of all:

1. The armies were facing each other on opposite sides of a valley.

There was a distinction between the two armies. There was no question as to which army a person served because of the distance between the two sides. Today, the forces of darkness are gathered to wage war with us. And just as plainly as there were two distinct sides in David's time, so there are two distinct camps in our own day. We cannot be in both armies. We are either serving in the army of God or in the army of Satan. A middle-of-the-road position might serve a person running for office, but it doesn't impress the Lord at all. In fact, He would rather we be hot for Him (running after Him with fervency) or totally cold for Him (completely self-absorbed), because lukewarmness in serving God is completely unacceptable. He will vomit the fence-sitters out of His mouth and consequently out of His presence. (Revelation 3:16).

In Exodus we read of Moses' realization that without God's presence all was hopeless. Moses presented himself and the people to the Lord and asked for God's special favor upon them:

> *"And He said, 'My Presence will go with you, and I will give you rest.'*
> *The he said to Him, 'If Your Presence does not go with us, do not bring us up from here'"*
> Exodus 33:14-15.

What wisdom! Lord, don't even bother to send us out unless You are going ahead. Praise God we can not only expect that He will send us out, but that His Spirit will attend us every step of the way.

God's Presence Makes All the Difference!

The presence of God is what separates the people of God from the rest of the world. Without God dwelling among us, we are no different from anyone else. But when God chooses to tabernacle or live within our hearts we are suddenly elevated to a supernatural existence that makes us come out from our old lives and walk in newness of faith. It's called sanctification. Paul writes on this principle in Corinthians:

> *"Do not be unequally yoked together with unbelievers. For what fellowship has righteousness with lawlessness? And what communion has light with darkness?*
> *And what accord has Christ with Belial? Or what part has a believer with an unbeliever?*

And what agreement has the temple of God with idols? For you are the temple of the living God. As God has said: 'I will dwell in them and walk among them. I will be their God, and they shall be My people.'

Therefore, 'Come out from among them and be separate, says the Lord. Do not touch what is unclean, and I will receive you. I will be a Father to you, and you shall be My sons and daughters, says the Lord Almighty'" II Corinthians 6:14-18.

Notice that even though God promises to dwell among us and personally infill us, it is based upon our decision to be separated from the unclean things of this world. God will never force His presence upon anyone; He will not intrude upon a life which does not desire His presence. But, when we allow Him to clean up our lives and we choose to separate ourselves unto Him (it's called consecration), He promises to go with us and empower us to run the race. The first observation we make regarding the story of David is that the two armies faced each other and were distinct from one another.

2.   There was a valley between them.

A valley in the Bible often represents more than simply an indention in the geography between two higher points. Sometimes a valley represents a spiritual challenge; other times it represents a place of uncertainty, such as "the valley of the shadow of death" in Psalm 23, a place of darkness and mystery through which God promises to accompany us. The prophet Joel speaks of a valley of decision wherein multitudes of people are called upon to decide one way or the other as to whom they will serve:

*"Multitudes, multitudes in the valley of decision!
For the day of the Lord is near in the valley of decision"* Joel 3:14.

The valley represents a combination of these to the two
opposing armies. For Israel the valley represents an uneasy
buffer between themselves and the enemy. It is a place from
where they can't get hurt, but where they can't do much
damage to the enemy either. Sometimes Christians come
to a point in their lives where they prefer a valley between
themselves and the enemy rather than risk a position on
the front lines. During the trench warfare of World War I,
the area between the trenchworks of the two armies was
called "No man's land." It was a place claimed by neither
side, but was vulnerable to attack should a soldier from one
of the armies venture out into it. Sometimes there was something of value that both armies wanted, like a live milk cow
or some chickens that wandered out onto the battlefield
and the contest was on to see which side would prevail in
getting the prize for their side. Both sides would cheer on
their men as first one, and then another side, would send
someone out to run after the cow to force it to their own
lines. Christians need to realize that there are prizes to be
taken in the valleys we face and that God is not only cheer-
ing us on from behind, but is out on the field with us!
Pacesetters go into the valley to do their fighting!

3. **The enemy was occupying ground that belonged
   to the people of God.**
   The Philistine army was holding ground that did not
belong to them; it belonged to Judah. We need to recognize
that the enemy has made unwarranted intrusions into our
lives and the lives of others because we have allowed him
entrance. If we can just recognize that we are fighting to

retake what God has already given to us, we will fight with greater intensity.

One of the great motivations for the Crusaders during the Middle Ages was to retake the Holy Land from the Moslem conquerors. As the armies of Europe approached Jerusalem, their banners with Christian symbols fluttered in the wind. After terrific battle, they retook Jerusalem and held it for a few years, as well as other sites deemed holy to Christendom. Were all of the participants in these bloody battles upright, pure men of God? Of course not! Some were in it for adventure, some for gold, some because they had no choice—but some viewed the wars as a holy cause. The point was not the individuals participating being in and of themselves perfect as much as the calling—a crusade for the glory of God! As Christians, we must realize that people rally to a cause when they believe it is worthwhile. Pacesetters must represent Christ as the most worthy cause in which a person can be involved. Many Christians who are lukewarm will see the passion and begin to live their faith with renewed vigor. (This is precisely what happens to Saul's army after David's encounter with Goliath—but more on that later!) Crusades are contagious, and hazardous, to the enemy's health!

Nine Feet Of Sheer Intimidation

"And a champion went out from the camp of the Philistines, named Goliath, from Gath, whose height was six cubits and a span.

He had a bronze helmet on his head, and he was armed with a coat of mail, and the weight of the coat was five thousand shekels of bronze.

And he had a bronze armor on his legs and a bronze javelin between his shoulders.

Now the staff of his spear was like a weaver's beam, and his iron spearhead weighed six hundred shekels; and a shield-bearer went before him" I Samuel 17:4-7.

Fearful opposition always gets a response. Even the most faith-filled, radical Christian can be rattled if only for a moment. The demonic world is good at instilling fear; in fact, they thrive on it. Fear is one of the most potent weapons in the enemy's arsenal. If he can keep a person off-balance because of being afraid, he has completely immobilized him (or at least slowed him way down).

Fear comes in many flavors, from outright terror by demonic visitations to more subtle fears such as fear of failure, fear to witness, fear to take a risk. When Franklin Roosevelt came to office in 1933, the country was in a deep depression, both economically and psychologically. FDR knew that he had to get the people focused on the possibilities rather than to dwell on the current realities.

During his inaugural speech, as he described the challenges that America faced, he uttered these famous words: "The only thing we have to fear, is fear itself." Everything else was possible to deal with, he said. But fear would only lead to further panic and greater erosion of the society. Here was a man who was an invalid; he could not walk as a result of infantile paralysis which he succumbed to at 39. The man in the wheelchair was leading the nation. If anyone knew about fear and the challenges therein, it was this man. He once remarked that, "If you have spent two years in bed trying to wiggle your big toe, everything else seems easy."[1]

So who was this Goliath? He was a big man to say the least. Let's run down his stats:

Height:	Nine feet, nine inches	
Weight:	Approximately 500 - 600 pounds	
Armor:	Coat of mail:	125 pounds
	Helmet :	10 pounds
	Leg greaves:	20 pounds
	Breastplate:	20 pounds
	Spearhead:	15 pounds
	Sword:	10 pounds
	Shields:	<u>30 pounds</u>
Total weight of outerwear:		230 pounds

This guy was a walking tank, and he probably had the brains to match. He was nine feet nine inches of ugly wrapped up in heavy-duty weaponry. His name, "Goliath," means "soothsayer." A soothsayer is one who tells the future. This is exactly what fear tries to do to us—dictate our future by telling us how things are in the present. "You can't do that!"; "You've tried that before!"; "She isn't going to listen to you!" and on and on. **Fear tries to foul up our future by paralyzing our present.** This is exactly what Goliath was doing to the army of Saul.

> *"Then he stood and cried out to the armies of Israel, and said to them, 'Why have you come out to line up for battle? Am I not a Philistine, and you the servants of Saul? Chose a man for yourselves, and let him come down to me.*
>
> *If he is able to fight with me and kill me, then we will be your servants. But if I prevail against him and kill him, then you shall be our servants and serve us.'*
>
> *And the Philistine said, 'I defy the armies of Israel this day; give me a man, that we may fight together.'*

When Saul and all Israel heard these words of the Philistine, they were dismayed and greatly afraid. Now David was the son of that Ephrathite of Bethlehem Judah, whose name was Jesse, and who had eight sons. And the man was old, advanced in years, in the days of Saul" I Samuel 17:8-12.

Who wouldn't be? Nobody in their natural mind would consider going head to head with this giant. However, a challenge was issued and a response needed to be made. The contest was quite clear: somebody must go down and fight the giant—not only fight him, but kill him. Those were his terms. But who?

There are some interesting ideas that Goliath brings up. I hate to credit the giant with something true, but he points out some principles in his challenge that cannot be overlooked:

1. **The people of God are dressed for battle but no body is fighting.**

Goliath is basically asking Saul's army what their intention is—fight or not? Many Christians look good in the ranks: arms lifted in worship, Bibles open during sermons, always in attendance. Yet, if you put some of these people on the battlelines, their real spiritual confidence bleeds through. We can put all the spiritual armor on that we want, from the helmet of salvation to the shield of faith, but if we are unwilling to do battle when the day of battle comes, we are about as useful as a flat tire. One time King Ahab answered a challenge from the king of Syria this way, *"Let not him who girds (puts) on his armor boast like him who takes it off" (I Kings 20:11) NAS.* Until our armor is tested in battle, we have proven nothing.

2. **The contest is winner takes all; there are no second places.**

Notice the challenge: If you fight and win, you will conquer us. If we fight and defeat you, we will conquer you. There are no other considerations. This is an all or nothing contest between the people of God and the people of darkness. It is a fight to the death which has been won by the death and resurrection of our Lord.

Through death, Jesus conquered death for us and destroyed forever the power of the devil to rule our lives. Jesus has brought to us the power of His Word and the Holy Spirit to defeat the works of the enemy in our lives and in the lives of others. How did he secure this? *OBEDIENCE*! Because Jesus was obedient, even to the point of agonizing death on the cross, we have victory.

> *"For as by one man's (Adam's) disobedience many were made sinners, so also by one Man's (Jesus') obedience many will be made righteous"* Romans 5:19.

3. **When the leadership is afraid, everyone is effected.**

Instead of setting the pace for his people, Saul is quaking in his tent. As a result, everybody in the camp is infected with fear. If we are to be Pacesetters, we have to be the ones who will stand up and take on the challenge. Somebody must answer the boastful challenges of the enemy! By the way, if the current leaders will not take up God's cause, He will find someone else with the faith to fight.

4. **Fear can never really harm you.**

In all of the shouting, and walking up and down the lines that Goliath did, not one person was actually physically harmed. Fear can only hurt you if you allow it to enter into your heart and mind. Not one real weapon had been used at this point, only words. As we'll find out, words are a devastating weapon that can be used for a person when delivered in faith, or can destroy a person when received in fear.

The Power of Spoken Words

Somebody once said that "the pen is mightier than the sword." This little proverb illustrates the power of words. Words can move a nation to action, cause a situation to reverse itself, increase faith and give confidence. They can also tear down, discourage and paralyze. As Christians we recognize that our words, when backed up by the truth of Scripture and by faith, are the most powerful weapon we possess. Paul says:

> *"For the weapons of our warfare are not carnal but mighty in God for pulling down strongholds, casting down arguments and every high thing that exalts itself against the knowledge of God, bringing every thought into captivity to the obedience of Christ,"*
> II Corinthians 10:4-5.

How do we destroy these enemy strongholds? Through the spiritual weapons we possess, our words engaging our faith. Paul says it is a combination of the Holy Spirit and our faith which is effective, a combining of *"spiritual thoughts with spiritual words"* (I Corinthians 2:13) NAS.

We might be able to speak with the eloquence of Cicero, but unless those words are anchored in the truth of God, they are fleshly and useless. We should not attempt anything without knowing whether or not God is blessing that endeavor.

Benjamin Franklin gives a terrific illustration of just that point. When the Constitutional Convention was meeting in 1787, a crisis over what relationship the states would have toward each other threatened to break up the assembly.

Franklin (who was 81) delivered a speech to the convention in which he reminded the delegates that God must be recognized in all of the deliberations. At one point he said:

> *"I have lived, sir, a long time, and the longer I live the more convincing proofs I see of this truth—that God governs in the affairs of men. And if a sparrow cannot fall to the ground without his notice, is it probable that an empire can rise without His aid?"*[2]

The result was a complete change in attitude at the convention. One delegate, Jonathan Dayton of New Jersey, described Franklin's words as "even greater than what we may suppose an oracle to have had in the Roman Senate"[3]

A revival of sorts broke out as well. A motion followed by the convention president, James Madison, and seconded by Roger Sherman that:

> *"...a sermon be preached at the request of the convention on the 4th of July, the anniversary of independence; and thenceforward prayers be used in ye convention every morning."*[4]

Prayers have opened both houses of Congress ever since! All this came about as a result of very eloquent words spoken by an elderly gentleman. He was a great *pacesetter* for our country.

Giant Threats

On hearing the words of Goliath, backed up by the impression of strength which he demonstrated, the people of God sank back. The Bible account says that everyone was dismayed. This word in the Hebrew translates into the idea of a complete breakdown in attitude and spirit because of fear and confusion. To be dismayed is to be discouraged;

literally, to have the courage nullified within you and to be terrified.

Goliath certainly was scoring points in the intimidation department. For 40 days he railed against the army of Saul, holding them in a state of immobility because they were afraid of the things he was saying. The power of the enemy in our lives is in his ability to get us to listen to him and believe him. It started in Eden and he has been doing it ever since. Jesus said of Satan:

> "*He was a murderer from the beginning and does not stand in the truth, because there is no truth in him. When he speaks a lie, he speaks from his own resources, for he is a liar and the father of it*"
> John 8:44.

The enemy is a liar. Even when he mixes elements of truth with his suggestions to us he is masquerading a lie. It is his nature. We should not be taken by surprise when he comes to us with all manner of bad news. He's an expert at confusion, discouragement and fear. Many a good man and woman have fallen victim to his devices. In fact, one time the enemy even took me out to lunch one day. I had just arrived in Marysville, Washington where I had taken the Youth Pastor position. There was a young man who went to lunch with me at a local sandwich shop. After having some small talk and getting to know him, this young man began to give me the bad news. He looked at me and with a smirk on his face said, "Pastor Benny you're a nice guy and all, but I am telling you that you will not make a difference up here." I sat there in utter shock wondering if I was really hearing what I thought I was hearing. This young man said there were too many drugs and too much partying going on for me to think I was going to bring about a change. His words hit deep within my spirit as I was grasping the intent of the enemy. The enemy wanted to paralyze me with the words of this young man. I sat and thought for a moment and then I responded. I said, "You're absolutely right I cannot make a difference but Jesus will." Praise God! The lies of the enemy had tried to rob me, but inspired me instead to cling to the truth of God's Word. Needless to say, God proved that young man wrong as we saw the youth Church grow to over 500 students with hundreds being radically changed by the power of God.

As Pacesetters, we are to expose the lies of the enemy and shed light on his intruding darkness. We are to speak the truth in love and set the record straight that Jesus is the Way, the Truth and the Life. But remember, the only way we can speak the truth is to know the truth—by reading God's Word and making it a part of our lives.

1. Jon Johnstone, Christian Excellence, (Grand Rapids: Baker Book House, 1995), p. 94.
2. Ronald H. Bailey, The Home Front: USA, (Alexandria, Va.: Time-Life Books, Inc., 1978) p. 18.
3. William J. Federer, America's God and Country, (Coppell, Texas: FAME Publishing, 1994), p.248.
4. Ibid, p. 249.
5. Ibid, p. 249.

Chapter Five

...the Harder They Fall

> "Worry is really a negative prayer—prayer in re-
> verse—that can bring upon us exactly what we do
> not want and fear the most."[1]
>
> From "The Seven Spiritual Secrets of
> Success" by Richard Briley

We just learned that the enemy is great at causing distraction and discouragement. If he can keep Christians off
balance by being afraid or fighting amongst ourselves, he
knows he is in control of the situation. He already has non-
Christians buying into his lies so he doesn't need to concern himself with them as much. And so he presents a challenge; a circumstance; a giant to us and threatens us and
asks what we intend to do about it.

Enter David

Thankfully our Lord is never taken by surprise by anything. When the enemy raises up a challenger, you can be sure that God will raise up a defender—a Pacesetter—who will rise to the confrontation. This follows all the way through the Bible:

Moses vs Pharaoh
Joshua vs the Canaanite kings
David vs Goliath
Esther vs Haman
And more!

The point is that God will raise up anyone who is willing to demonstrate the faith and will to be His champion. He does not care about physical appearance, intellectual prowess or economic strength. He is looking for a man or woman who is after His own heart. So it is with David.

"Now David was the son of that Ephrathite of Bethlehem Judah, whose name was Jesse, and who had eight sons. And the man was old, advanced in years, in the days of Saul.

The three oldest sons of Jesse had gone to follow Saul to the battle. The names of his three sons who went to the battle were Eliab the firstborn, next to him Abinadab, and the third Shammah.

David was the youngest. And the three oldest followed Saul.

But David occasionally went and returned from Saul to feed his father's sheep at Bethlehem"
I Samuel 17:12-15.

We already looked at Goliath's stats. Now let's take a look at David's. First of all, he was a boy of around 14 to 15 years of age. He was the youngest of eight brothers and helped his father with the animals. He also was an errand boy, running back and forth between the battle site and his dad's flock.

But David had something going for him that neither his father, nor his brothers, nor Goliath, nor even Samuel realized fully: **David knew God.** He had a private life which was filled with worship and honor and love for the Lord which he had nourished during some of those quiet evenings tending the flocks. When Samuel came to anoint one of Jesse's sons as king, all the other sons were rejected. David was not even among the group during the initial selection; he was tending the herds! But the Lord said to Samuel as he stood before Eliab, first-born of the seven sons:

> *"Do not look at his appearance or at his physical stature, because I have refused him. For the Lord does not see as a man sees; for man looks at the outward appearance, but the Lord looks at the heart"*
> I Samuel 16:7.

One by one the Lord rejected Jesse's sons until He commanded that David be brought in. When David came from tending the flock the Lord said, *"Arise, anoint him; for this is he" (I Samuel 16:12) NAS.* You or I would have anointed big, bad Eliab. But God saw something in David that was far more valuable than physical ability. He saw inner strength. He saw a Pacesetter in the making!

Meanwhile Back at the Front...

On one of his errands to his brothers on the battlelines, David was talking with some of the men when Goliath came forward with his daily challenge. David was confused by the fear he saw in the men around him and asked what would be done for the man who killed the giant. He learned that King Saul had promised a huge reward to whoever would kill the giant. Not only would Jesse's taxes be dismissed forever, but David himself would be paid handsomely and would gain the hand of one of Saul's daughters in marriage.

This seemed like the chance of a lifetime to the young shepherd! Suddenly he heard the familiar voice of his oldest brother, Eliab, accusing him of being a busybody who only wanted to watch other men do battle. (Of course, if Eliab had taken a look around him he would have seen that as of yet nobody was doing any fighting!) David defended himself and continued asking about the reward, until the matter came to Saul's attention, who sent for David.

One of the benefits of being a Pacesetter is that there are special rewards for those who exercise special faith:

> *"But without faith it is impossible to please Him, for he who comes to God must believe that He is, and that He is a rewarder of those who diligently seek Him"* Hebrews 11:6.

> *"So Jesus answered and said, 'Assuredly, I say to you, there is no one who has left house or brothers or sisters or father or mother or wife or children or lands, for My sake and the gospel's, who shall not receive a hundredfold now in this time—houses and brothers and sisters and mothers and children and lands, with persecutions—and in the age to come, eternal life'"* Mark 10:29-30.

David recognized something that nobody else recognized in the camp. He realized that Goliath was not just taunting the army of Israel, but he was insulting the honor and name of the Lord Most High. The enemy was defying God and not man! He was simply using this occasion as a vehicle to get across his point of defiance. Shakespeare said, "the world was a stage and we are merely players in the drama of life." We are involved in the greatest chess match in the cosmos being played out right here on earth between light and darkness. We are players in the drama and by our faith we can help bring victory to our side! By offending the name of God, the enemy crossed over into dangerous territory. David refused to stand by and see the name of His God belittled by a mere giant. Pacesetters do not let an offense to their Lord go unanswered.

How could David, as untested in war as Goliath was skilled, even think of taking up the challenge of the enemy? Because he understood an underlying principle born out of his relationship with God; **he could trust God to deliver him and fight for him.** He had experienced God's intervention before and knew that what God had performed once, He would perform again. He told Saul:

> *"'Let no man's heart fail because of him; your servant will go and fight with this Philistine.'*
>
> *And Saul said to David, 'You are not able to go against this Philistine to fight with him; for you are a youth, and he a man of war from his youth.'*
>
> *But David said to Saul, 'Your servant used to keep his father's sheep, and when a lion or a bear came and took a lamb out of the flock, I went out after it and struck it, and delivered the lamb from its mouth; and when it arose against me, I caught it by its beard, and struck and killed it.*
>
> *Your servant has killed both lion and bear; and this uncircumcised Philistine will be like one of them, seeing he has defied the armies of the living God'"* 1 Samuel 17:32-36.

David had experienced God in personal struggles before. He saw all of his life as preparatory for this moment and believed that God would deliver him in this battle as well. He knew he could trust God and place his faith in Him based upon his experiences in the past. Pacesetter principles are evident in David's attitude:

1. Pacesetters know and accept responsibility.

More importantly, God knew that he could trust David. Here was a young man who had proven himself faithful in the little things—tending the sheep late at night when everyone else was asleep. When we prove ourselves to God, he proves Himself in us. *If we are to be Pacesetters, we must accept whatever responsibility, great or small, that God sets before us. No job is too little to be done responsibly before the Lord.*

2. Pacesetters rely on the Lord for their strength.

David realized from where his strength came. The Lord was the one who enabled him to kill the lion and bear and He would do the same with Goliath. *Pacesetters know from where their power comes.*

3. Pacesetters recognize their uniqueness to God and His methods.

When Saul offered David his armor and weapons, David could not wear them. For one thing they didn't fit. Besides that, God had another plan for the battle. David could not wear the armor of another man anymore than he could depend upon another man to deliver him in this situation. The faith of others will not get us into heaven. This is what I am talking about when I speak of having a first-hand revelatory encounter with Jesus. David understood that God would bring the victory as he fought as himself—not as Saul.

We must recognize that God has purposely made us different, with different gifts and abilities, and allow God to take advantage of our uniqueness to His glory. The big mistake that Christians often make is trying to be somebody they are not. This is not only insulting to God's purpose in individual design, but can lead to big trouble if a person gets off into the wrong ministries. God knows exactly what He is doing with us. Let's make a list of principles that David has taught us thus far:

1. **We must be prepared with both past experiences with God as well as putting on the full armor of God— God's armor, not ours.**

   "Put on the whole armor of God, that you may be able to stand against the wiles of the devil" Ephesians 6:11.

   We need to allow God's spiritual armor to protect and keep us. The reason why we cannot wear another's armor is because we have to maintain our own faith. I cannot be saved by another man's faith anymore than I can be protected by another man' s spiritual armor. My faith is what allows me to put the armor on in the first place, not someone else's.

2. **We must be prepared to do battle God's way and not man's way.**
   Saul was only trying to help by offering David his personal armor, but David understood that he could only fight the way God had taught him. We must do things God's way! Proverbs says:

   "There is a way that seems right to a man, but its end is the way of death" Proverbs 14:12.

   Pacesetters never act on what "seems" right; rather, they act upon the truth of God's Word regardless of how it might feel. Faith is action, not feeling.

3. David chose the basics for the battle.

David relied on the tried and true elements of the faith, not on the untested armor of Saul. He was familiar with his sling and a few stones; anything else was unnecessary. We also must rely on the basics to fight the enemy successfully. What are these? Here are a few of the basic implements we need to carry as we come against the enemy:

Prayer

Worship   Bible study

Witnessing   Fellowship   Servanthood

Giving   Intercession   Healing   Discipleship   Encouragement

There are countless other weapons in our arsenal. President Woodrow Wilson called the might and industrial power of the United States during World War One the "arsenal of democracy." The spiritual weapons of our warfare might be called the arsenal of *theocracy*, because God is our ruler and we are citizens of His kingdom using His weaponry. Talk about an arms race!

The Point of Confrontation

When everything is said and done, and all the preparations have been made, there comes a point when the actual conflict must occur. Usually the conflict has been raging way in advance in the spiritual realm before it ever explodes into the physical world. In fact the confrontation began in the spiritual world when Satan foolishly thought he could usurp God's position. It has been a titanic struggle ever since, though a foregone conclusion as to the winner.

The fight was on as David and Goliath drew near to each other:

> *"Then he took his staff in his hand; and he chose for himself five smooth stones from the brook, and put them in a shepherd's bag, in a pouch which he had, and his sling was in his hand. And he drew near to the Philistine.*
>
> *So the Philistine came, and began drawing near to David, and the man who bore the shield went before him.*
>
> *And when the Philistine looked about and saw David, he disdained him; for he was only a youth, ruddy and good-looking.*
>
> *So the Philistine said to David, 'Am I a dog, that you come to me with sticks?' And the Philistine cursed David by his gods.*
>
> *And the Philistine said to David, 'Come to me, and I will give your flesh to the birds of the air and the beasts of the field!'"* I Samuel 17:40-44.

The Bible uses a very interesting word in describing Goliath's harassment of David. The text says he "disdained" him. The meaning here is to dis-esteem or put down in ridicule. Goliath was basically viewing David as a non-threat and even an insult to someone of his stature. Pride often blinds a person's ability to assess the strength of the opposition. Goliath used the weapons of fear, intimidation and doubt by telling David that he was a mere distraction to the main event. David apparently had other ideas:

> *"Then David said to the Philistine, 'You come to me with a sword, with a spear, and with a javelin. But I come to you in the name of the Lord of hosts, the God of the armies of Israel, whom you have defied.*

*This day the Lord will deliver you into my hand,
and I will strike you and take your head from you.
And this day I will give the carcasses of the camp of
the Philistines to the birds of the air and the wild beasts
of the earth, that all the earth may know that there is
a God in Israel.*

*Then all this assembly shall know that the Lord
does not save with sword and spear; for the battle is
the Lord's, and He will give you into our hands'"* I
Samuel 17:45-47.

Notice that David does not deny the reality of the problem and in fact, he names off the advantages of the enemy he is about to confront: sword, spear, javelin. We cannot deny the power of the enemy, that would be foolish. In fact, Paul says *"we are not ignorant of his (Satan's) schemes" (II Corinthians 2:11) NAS.* But just because we are aware of the enemy's power, it is a mistake to dwell upon it and give him glory. I believe we Christians give Satan a lot more credit than he deserves by talking about how strong he is.

The Name of the Lord

David had at his disposal the greatest weapon one can possibly have when it is engaged with faith: the name of the Lord (and all the authority that name represents). Let's review some scriptures about the name of the Lord. Philippians 2 introduces the idea of the supremacy of God's name:

*"Therefore God also has highly exalted Him and
given Him the name which is above every name, that
at the name of Jesus every knee should bow, of those
in heaven, and of those on earth, and of those under
the earth, and that every tongue should confess that*

Jesus Christ is Lord, to the glory of God the Father"
Philippians 2:9-11.

Mark describes a number of possibilities for those who
believe and speak in the name of Jesus:

> *"...in My name they will cast out demons; they*
> *will speak with new tongues;*
> *they will take up serpents; and if they drink any-*
> *thing deadly, it will by no means hurt them; they will*
> *lay hands on the sick, and they will recover"*
> Mark 16:17-18.

I have personally seen the power of the name of Jesus in
action. One time while I was ministering in Washington a
young lady was demon possessed. Some of my workers took
her to a back room where they were going to do deliverance. After a short time I decided to go back to where the
deliverance was taking place. The girl was very violent as
the demon was demonstrating demonic power through her.
As I entered the room the young lady rose to her feet and
the demons raged at me. The young lady was threatening
to kill me. At that moment I looked at the demonized girl
and quoted Philippians 2:9-11 which says that at the name
of Jesus everything must bow. So I said to the demon, "in
Jesus' name bow you knee." Immediately the girl fell to her
knees and could not get up again. That night I truly recognized that the name of Jesus is truly the name above all
names!
The 11th chapter of Hebrews is commonly called the
"hall of faith" because of the list of tremendous deeds performed in faith by great men and women of the Bible through
the power of the Lord and in His name:

"...who through faith subdued kingdoms, worked righteousness, obtained promises, stopped the mouths of lions, quenched the violence of fire, escaped the edge of the sword, out of weakness were made strong, became valiant in battle, turned to flight the armies of the aliens" Hebrews 11:33-34.

God's Name Brings Confidence

David had total confidence in victory. Why? Because he was fighting in the name of the Lord and according to God's plan. He knew that the greater outcome was not the death of a nine foot tall megalomaniac, but that God would be glorified. Two things would happen as a result of David's obedience:

1.   **The world will know there is a God.**
2.   **People will know that God does not save by carnal means.**

Pacesetters run toward the battle, not away from it. But they also realize that there' is a time and a place for a battle; engaging the enemy is not to be done in a foolish or frivolous manner. (Remember the seven sons of Sceva?)

Victory!

David was as good as his prophecy. He not only knocked Goliath out cold with his little sling, but he took the giant's sword and cut off his head. When the armies saw what had happened, there was a breakthrough for the army of Saul. The Philistines panicked and retreated into their own territory and Israel won a mighty victory. The occupied territory was recovered, and the Philistines were humbled until another day.

What are some observations we can make about this wonderful account in I Samuel?

1. **Victory is assured, but we must be willing to step out in faith and face our problems.**

   God has promised us the win if we take the risk of faith to believe on His name. Read Hebrew 11 and you'll see a whole list of people who moved the world because they believed in God's victory.

2. **We must be willing to face the giants in our lives.**

   Unless we learn that problems will not just "go away" and begin to face and dispose of them, we will get nowhere fast. The greater things of God often depend upon our ability to deal with the lesser problems which we all face.

3. **We must be willing to take a stand, even if nobody else does.**

   David alone volunteered to fight the giant. Sometimes you may be the only one of the group who has a chance to make a difference. What will you do?

4. **We must focus on the Father, our victorious leader.**

   The Bible says we are to *"fix our eyes on Jesus, the author and perfecter of faith" (Hebrews 12:2) NAS,* and not turn to the left or right. Jesus must be our focus as we move ahead in faith. He's not our light at the end of the tunnel; He's our light *in* the tunnel!

5. **We must flow in the power of the Holy Spirit.**

   It wasn't David's skill as a slingshot marksman that killed Goliath. The power that propelled that little stone deep into the giant's forehead was the Holy Spirit. We must partner with the Spirit of God if we are going to succeed. As we step out in faith, the Holy Spirit will enable us to be bold and speak the word of truth to whatever situation we encounter. Remember what the Bible admonishes in Zechariah: *"Not) by might, nor by power, but by My Spirit," says the Lord of Hosts" (Zechariah 4:6) NAS.* The next time you meet up with a nine foot, nine inch giant who thinks you are nothing but a distraction, remember that the battle belongs to the Lord. So...

Step Up to the Fight,

Step Aside for the Lord,

Step On the Giant's Head

---

1. Richard Briley, <u>The Seven Spiritual Secrets of Success</u> (Nashville, TN; Thomas Nelson Publishers, 1995), p. 146

Chapter Six

Isaiah the Pacesetter

> *"(Spiritual authority and leadership) is not won by promotion, but by many prayers and tears. It is attained by confession of sin, and much heart searching and humbling before God; by self-surrender, a courageous sacrifice of every idol, a bold uncomplaining embrace of the cross, and by an eternal and unfaltering looking unto Jesus crucified. It is not gained by seeking great things for ourselves, but like Paul, by counting those things that are gain to us as loss for Christ. This is a great price, but it must be paid by the leader who would not be merely a nominal but a real spiritual leader of men, a leader whose power is recognized and felt in heaven, on earth, and in hell."[1]*

From "The Soul-Winner's Secret"
by Samuel Brengle

In the previous chapter I introduced the idea of being Pacesetters, which are, Christians who are setting the standard and not following the trend. We looked at David, who set the pace for a tremendous victory by stepping out in faith and killing the giant, rather than following the trend of fear that was keeping the people of God from moving forward. I also outlined five concepts that we should remember when we are in the valley preceding the battle:

1. **Pacesetters face their problem.**
2. **Pacesetters go to God for their strength.**
3. **Pacesetters stand in the battle (Ephesians 6).**
4. **Pacesetters focus on the Father.**
5. **Pacesetters flow in the Spirit.**

We also followed the development of David from forgotten shepherd boy to champion of Israel. David clearly set the pace for his generation and changed the course of history. In this chapter we're going to examine another man who took up the challenge as a pacesetter for his generation: the prophet Isaiah.

With the possible exception of Moses' burning bush experience, no other biblical character has as dramatic a call into service for the Lord as Isaiah. Face to face with the Almighty, Isaiah encounters not only the holiness of God, but the unholiness of his own life. Yet in the mystery of God's grace, Isaiah, flawed as he is in his own right, is commissioned to preach the word of the Lord to an unruly and unreceptive people. Isaiah's story is encouraging to all of us, because there is a clear reminder that God will use anyone who is repentant and willing.

Isaiah certainly is not perfect when he sees the Lord in the temple; and David probably wouldn't have impressed us very much upon his appearance at the battlelines; and we often snicker at Peter's miscalculated enthusiasm. Guess what? You and I are not perfect either. But the same God who cleaned up and commissioned Isaiah; the same God who enabled a "nobody" shepherd boy to become king; the same God who told Peter that "upon this rock I will build my church"; is the same God that calls us to set the pace for our generation.

Taking it on the Chin

It's common to hear people complain about how tough it is to minister to this ungrateful, self-indulgent society. Examples of attitude toward ministering to an unreceptive world which spring to mind include: "Nobody is interested in God anymore"; or "Either people are too steeped in sin to change, or too religious not to change"; or how about this one: "These people deserve exactly what's coming to them but I'm going to minister to them anyway!" I recall a cartoon in which a minister is hiding under his desk as a parishioner attempts to see him about a problem. (Probably happens more than we realize!)

Perhaps more significant is the reality of an anti-Christian bias in our culture which seeks to demean and weaken authentic Christianity. Where once clergy were given a measure of respect because of their calling, now they are many times objects of sitcom humor and talk-show scandals. I must admit that there have been some very obvious high-profile ministries which have fueled the flames of criticism, but I am talking about a general cultural contempt aimed at professional ministers and directly toward the church in America. Those who espouse a watered-down version of the gospel which is inclusive and compromising are hailed as great humanitarians, while the steadfast men and women of God who will not bend to cultural and social trends are railed as bigots or intolerant extremists.

Add to this the fact that many denominations are actually losing more vocational ministers than they are gaining. Many pastors are underpaid and unappreciated as they shoulder the burden of their churches. Others have allowed personal feelings of insecurity interfere with their leadership. The result is stress in the home, inability to follow through in their ministry tasks, and eventual burnout. More and more pastors are resigning churches in an attempt to find a more satisfying position; many are leaving the ministry altogether. (Perhaps this would be a good place for you to stop for a moment and pray for your pastor!) You can see what a tough challenge Christians, both clergy and laity, face in bringing the good news to the '90's. But as Pacesetters we're in good company because the prophets had a pretty difficult ministry themselves!

Another Time, Another Place (But Not So Different)

Do you remember the old "Bullwinkle" cartoons, with Rocky the flying squirrel, Boris, Natasha and Fearless Leader, and of course, Bullwinkle the moose? There was a segment on the show in which a boy named Sherman would travel back in time with a little white dog named Mr. Peabody in an invention called the "Wayback Machine." I can't engineer a real time machine and take you with me, but I invite you to use your imagination and visit old Jerusalem, around 740 B.C., and investigate the field in which Isaiah ministered.

As we come in over the City of David we see much activity in the stony pavements below: street vendors hawking their goods; caravans entering and leaving the city; the normal hustle and bustle of urban life in the post-Bronze Age. Despite all of the noise and distractions, our attention is drawn to a wonderfully intricate building, massive in size and breath-taking in beauty: the Temple of Solomon. It's been about 280 years since the establishment of the kingdom of Israel under Saul, a little over 200 years since the reign of David, and about 180 years since Solomon ruled and built the great temple.

In Isaiah's time, life goes on in the temple as it has for many years. The priests continue to minister their sacred duties even though the sacredness has long since vanished. The heart and soul of God's covenant of loving faithfulness has been replaced by the legalistic regimen of a handful of men. Religion is very much alive in old Jerusalem, and loving faithfulness is very much dead.

In politics, the nation has corrupted itself. First, the country split in two following the reign of Solomon. Israel, the kingdom of the north, has only a few years before being swallowed up once and for all by Assyria in 722 B.C. Judah, the kingdom in which Jerusalem is situated, will survive a while longer before she too succumbs to earthly passions and corruption, and goes down in judgment at the hands of Babylon in 587 B.C.

The political situation at every level is appalling. Local leaders take bribes, judges rule unfairly, widows and orphans are left to starve, the rich are given every preference and there is no justice in the land.

Economically, it is a time of prosperity and uncertainty. The prophets decried the rich who were indolent and hedonistic at the expense of their fellow Israelites. Nobody wants to hear the bad news a prophet brings and, in fact, the kings often surround themselves with advisors and seers who tell them that all is well with the world. Being a true prophet is hazardous to one's health.

A corrupted, entrenched religion; a crooked political system; a prosperous and selfish upper class; and a nation which doesn't want to hear the truth: this is the mission field to which Isaiah is sent. Talk about having it tough in the 1990's! Enough of the setting; let's take a look at Isaiah himself and how God called him to set the pace for his nation.

Isaiah: Called to Be a *Pacesetter*

Isaiah was a man who was totally committed to God and speaking the words that God had given him to speak. Isaiah's name means, "The Lord is salvation," and is the same derivative of the name of many other outstanding biblical characters including Joshua, Josiah, Hosea and Jesus. Isaiah's ministry spanned the reigns of four kings in Judah: Uzziah, Jotham, Ahaz and Hezekiah. In his lifetime he saw the collapse of the northern kingdom of Israel and the pressing in of the enemies of God around the nation of Judah, as the people continued in their hardness toward the Lord.

His message was simple: **repent and turn to the Lord for your salvation.** Isaiah is closely linked with the ministry of Jesus because much of his prophetic writings deal with the coming Messiah. Many verses in the book of Isaiah speak about the person and work of Jesus, both in vivid description and in wonderful imagery. It is in Isaiah 53 where we find the description of the broken and disfigured Christ, who is barely recognizable because of the severe treatment he endures. Isaiah also describes the earthly ministry of Jesus in Chapter 61. The fingerprints of Messiah are all over this wonderful book!

God Calling

The call of God on one's life is one of those subjective, hard-to-describe experiences which want explanation, but for which there really is no definition. Apart from the obvious reality that we are all called by God to do some things, it is also a fact that some of us are called of God to do particular things. If you ask a dozen ministers about their call experience, you'll probably get twelve different scenarios describing that event. You'll probably also find at least one common theme running the course of the experiences: *an inner conviction which would not go away and which compelled these ministers to choose for God and His plan.* Sometimes it's called "surrendering to the ministry" and for good reason! Even though not all calls of God are as dramatic as the one we are about to study, the calling of men and women into the Lord's service, whatever that might be, is as meaningful an experience today as it was in Isaiah's time.

Isaiah's call in Chapter 6 is one of the most important sections of Scripture in the Old Testament. It's often taught in connection with a missions effort following the, *"Here I am, send me!"*, response. But Isaiah 6 also illustrates some important and practical concepts for those who would be Pacesetters some 2600 years later! We are allowed:

—a peek into the presence of God,
—a heavenly worship service in session,
—the impact of the presence of God on His servant, Isaiah.

We also are taught the appropriate response to God's presence in our own lives, and that it is God's presence which convicts, cleanses and commissions us for service unto Him.

The fact that the call of Isaiah doesn't take place until Chapter 6 causes some to wonder why the prophet isn't called by the Lord officially until well into his ministry. The first five chapters of Isaiah are actually a statement of God's case against the people of Judah and what His ultimate plan for Jerusalem involves. In God vs. the Nation of Judah, the Lord:

—condemns the people for not responding to His grace and goodness,
—calls the people rebellious and weighted down with iniquity,

—calls the sacrifices of the people worthless because there is no justice,

—calls the nation to repentance.

The first five chapters of Isaiah can be boiled down to this: **Religious activity is worthless if not coupled with true repentance.** What a setting for the prophet's call! These are the hard cases to whom Isaiah must minister. Who are the hard cases to whom *you* must minister? Let's read the text and discover the call of this Pacesetter-prophet.

"In the year that King Uzziah's died, I saw the Lord sitting on a throne, high and lifted up, and the train of His robe filled the temple" Isaiah 6:1.

While present at the great temple in Jerusalem, perhaps to worship the Lord, maybe to speak with the priests, or possibly to console himself on the recent death of Uzziah, Isaiah is caught up in a vision in which the Lord's throne room suddenly appears in the building. There are visual images of both the heavenly throne room and the temple structure itself in a blended picture, indicating that Isaiah is aware of his physical surroundings in the temple and the presence of God's throne within the temple at the same time.

The text begins with a historical footnote referencing the year of Uzziah's death, approximately 740 B.C. Uzziah's career had begun brilliantly as he promoted the worship of God, but ended tragically after an episode of pride which caused him to be struck with leprosy. (More on Uzziah in the next chapter!) Isaiah held the late king in high regard, as he had early-on been a proponent of Isaiah's reforms. The death of a king was as traumatic upon the people of ancient Israel as the death of a president is to us in the 20th century. It is a time of confusion and speculation, of wondering and waiting. Yet, we know that God remains firmly in control and desires that we cast our eyes toward heaven. Thus the Lord interrupted Isaiah's worship with this spectacular visitation.

The vivid contrast of the glorious Monarch in heaven to the reality of the dead king on earth is quite dramatic. God's vision is a reassurance of kingly authority which demonstrates that while on earth there may be the political turmoil and confusion associated with the death of a national leader; but in heaven there is sovereign control and all is well. We would do well to remember that no matter how rough things might be down on earth, God is still in control!

It is very interesting to note that Isaiah did not see God until King Uzziah died. There are many things in our lives that keep us from seeing God for who He really is. For Isaiah, the king was a super hero. King Uzziah was the most important thing in the prophet Isaiah's life. It took the removing of the one thing that was the most important aspect of Isaiah's life for him to see God. Many times it is the same way with us. **We need to remove the Uzziahs from our lives that would take our focus off of the Lord.**

I was challenged by the Lord one time about my love for Him. I prayed and told the Lord that I wanted nothing to come between Him and me. I had been dating a girl and did not realize what had taken place. My eyes had turned from putting the Lord first to having this lady first. My passion and desire for the Lord began to wain. The Lord took me to the story of Abraham and Isaac on the mountain of sacrifice. I felt the Lord speak to me that I needed to do the same thing and offer the one thing that I loved the most. So I was obedient and thought that the young lady would be spared and everything would be alright. However, God had other plans for me and her. We broke up and she went her way and I went mine. At the time I did not see why this turned out this way...but I focused upon God and began to see Him clearly then. I realize now as the years have gone by that God had other plans for her and me. Also He showed me that my eyes must be on Him and not on any "Uzziah's" that would hinder my sight.

The Bible makes it clear that the Lord is a jealous God and wants nothing to come before Him in our lives. In Matthew 22:37-40, Jesus makes it clear that we need to love the Lord with all our heart, soul, mind, and strength. Our love for God needs to be an all consuming passion that consumes us and our lives. That is what a Pacesetter is: **a person with an all consuming passion for God.** This will only happen when the Uzziahs are removed from our lives. Isaiah, after the death of Uzziah, says that he saw the Lord clearly like he has never seen Him before.

Isaiah gives us an eyewitness account as the vision unfolds before him. He says "I saw" (which in the Hebrew [ra'ah] means to see clearly) with a confidence that let's us know that he isn't just "seeing things," but he is seeing quite clearly and consciously. In other words, we can believe what he saw.

And what did he see?

1. The Lord seated on a throne. The name used for "Lord" in this verse is the Hebrew word "Adonai" which is an indication of rulership and majesty over His creation. It is a portrait of God's transcendence above and apart from all He has created. God is holy and separate from that which He has created. The majesty of God's train fills the temple. God's presence is inescapable even to the point of his robes flowing from His person.

Isaiah is given a clear view of who God is as the Lord presents Himself in majesty. It's quite an impressive description which defies the notion of God as "the man upstairs" with a long white beard, rosy cheeks, a grandfatherly pot belly and a Santa Claus disposition. The vision also puts to rest the idea that God is an "energy force," some vague presence which pulsates in our direction from time to time. God is a Person, not an old man, not energy, but a living Being with feelings, intelligence and personality. He is a richly complex individual who is incomprehensible, yet self-disclosing through His Person and His Word.

In the Revelation, John describes an event taking place around the throne of God which corroborates Isaiah's account. John supplies us with even greater detail of the heavenly courtroom:

"After these things I looked, and behold, a door standing open in heaven. And the first voice which I heard was like a trumpet speaking with me, saying, 'Come up here, and I will show you things which must take place after this.'

Immediately I was in the Spirit; and behold, a throne set in heaven, and One sat on the throne.

And He who sat there was like a jasper and a sardius stone in appearance; and there was a rainbow around the throne, in appearance like an emerald.

Around the throne were twenty-four thrones, and on the thrones I say twenty-four elders sitting, clothed in white robes; and they had crowns of gold on their heads.

And from the throne proceeded lightnings, thunderings, and voices. Seven lamps of fire were burning before the throne, which are the seven Spirits of God.

Before the throne there was a sea of glass, like crystal. And in the midst of the throne, and around the throne, were four living creatures full of eyes in front and in back.

The first living creature was like a lion, the second living creature like a calf, the third living creature had a face like a man, and the fourth living creature was like a flying eagle.

The four living creatures, each having six wings, were full of eyes around and within. And they do not rest day or night saying: 'Holy, holy, holy, Lord God Almighty, Who was and is and is to come!'

Whenever the living creatures give glory and honor and thanks to Him who sits on the throne, who lives forever and ever, the twenty-four elders fall down before Him who sits on the throne and worship Him who lives forever and ever, and cast their crowns before the throne, saying:

'You are worthy, O Lord, to receive glory and honor and power; for You created all things, and by Your will they exist and were created' " Revelation 4.

Isaiah's account is very similar to John's vision which indicates that they were looking at the same situation—the throne room of God. John is much more detailed in his description, but then Isaiah's vision was for a different purpose.

On With Isaiah

"Above it stood seraphim; each one had six wings: with two he covered his face, with two he covered his feet, and with two he flew" Isaiah 6:2.

2. He saw seraphim. A Seraph is an angelic being of high order. (Seraphim is the plural form of seraph.) The name means "burning one," perhaps reflecting the purity of God's presence and His glory which burns like fire. Notice their activity: They cover their feet and faces with two pairs of wings in humility and reverence, while the other set of wings is moving, ready to serve the Lord at a moment's notice.

"And one cried to another and said: 'Holy, holy, holy is the Lord of hosts; the whole earth is full of His glory!'
And the posts of the door were shaken by the voice of him who cried out, and the house was filled with smoke" Isaiah 6:3-4.

3. He saw them proclaim the Lord's holiness. So significant and vital is this truth that when the seraphim utter the words "holy," the temple itself begins to respond in convulsive recognition. Jesus said that if men did not praise the Father that the rocks would cry out in adoration. So it is with the temple as the Lord's holiness is called out by the angels.

In his book *The Pursuit of Holiness*, Jerry Bridges writes, "The absolute holiness of God should be of great comfort and assurance to us. If God is perfectly holy, then we can be confident that His actions toward us are always perfect and just."[2] "Because God is holy" means that He is always acting on our behalf. Many times we are tempted to believe that God is being unfair toward us. But the very fact that God is holy, gives us the assurance that God is always on our side, working out what is best for us. Why? Because He is holy and all His actions are pure and upright. **Take great assurance that the holiness of God provides great confidence that He is for you and not against you!**

Our problem is that we approach God casually not recognizing His holiness because we see Him through sin-tainted lenses. It is only as we are cleaned up that we can see how truly holy God is, and how truly far we have to go to be perfect as He is perfect. God's holiness:

—**signifies His absolute purity of character,**
—**sets Him apart from His creation,**
—**separates Him from sin,**
—**shows His opposition to evil.**

Perhaps for the first time in his life, Isaiah comes into meaningful contact with the holiness of the God he serves. By seeing God for who He is, Isaiah is able to more clearly see the man he has become. God cannot look upon sin, and therefore Isaiah feels the isolation sin causes. In his daily devotional, *Unto the Hills,* Billy Graham comments about God's inability to look upon sin:

> *"The Bible teaches us that God is holy, without fault, perfect and complete. From Genesis to Revelation, God reveals Himself as a holy God. He is so holy that He cannot endure sin, cannot even look upon it. It was God's holiness that caused Him to turn His back when the Lord Jesus Christ took upon Himself the sin of the entire world at Calvary. It was the only time in the eternal unity of the Trinity that God the Father and God the Son had a rupture in their relationship."[3]*

> *"So I said: 'Woe is me, for I am undone! Because I am a man of unclean lips, and I dwell in the midst of a people of unclean lips; for my eyes have seen the King, the Lord of hosts'"* Isaiah 6:5.

In view of God's holiness, Isaiah realizes his own imperfection and uncleanness. This is the first great lesson from Isaiah's call:

1. **When we come into the holy presence of God we will become convicted of any sin in our lives.**

God's presence brings conviction. It is as if standing in the presence of God places us under a spiritual microscope and magnifies those areas of our lives which need cleaning up.

Isaiah's particular problem centers on his speech. The Scripture doesn't indicate whether he is a chronic liar, or curses, or gossips. James tells us:

> *"Even so the tongue is a little member and boasts great things. See how great a forest a little fire kindles!*
> *And the tongue is a fire, a world of iniquity. The tongue is so set among our members that it defiles the whole body, and sets on fire the course of nature; and it is set on fire by hell.*
> *For every kind of beast and bird, of reptile and creature of the sea, is tamed and has been tamed by mankind.*
> *But no man can tame the tongue. It is an unruly evil, full of deadly poison"* James 3:5-8.

Sin cannot stand in the presence of God. It must be dealt with. Isaiah deals with his sin in the appropriate manner; he confesses it to the Lord. Sin will either seek to hide from God or will allow itself to be exposed. The second great lesson then from this story is:

2. The response to conviction of sin in our lives is confession.

We should never pass up an opportunity to get right with God when the Holy Spirit is convicting us. Conviction should always lead to confession! Isaiah was convicted of his sin by the presence of God and confessed it to Him. To confess means to own up to or admit something. Look how the Lord responds to Isaiah's confession:

"Then one of the seraphim flew to me, having in his hand a live coal which he had taken with the tongs from the altar.

And he touched my mouth with it, and said: 'Behold, this has touched your lips; your iniquity is taken away, and you sin purged'" Isaiah 6:6-7.

God responds to Isaiah's confession by cleansing him. This brings us to the third major truth in this section:

3. The act of confession on our part brings forgiveness and *cleansing* on God's part.

We know that only the blood of Jesus which was spilled 2000 years ago is strong and pure enough to pay the price for our forgiveness. In I John 1:9, we read, *"If we confess our sins, He is faithful and just to forgive us our sins, and to cleanse us from all unrighteousness." (NAS)* Other Scriptures which illustrate the work of cleansing which Christ effects for us include:

"...for all have sinned and fall short of the glory of God, being justified freely by His grace by the redemption that is in Christ Jesus" Romans 3:23-24.

"And according to the law almost all things are purified with blood, and without shedding of blood there is no remission" Hebrews 9:22.

"knowing that you were not redeemed with corruptible things, like silver or gold, from your aimless conduct received by tradition from your fathers, but with the precious blood of Christ, as of a lamb without blemish and without spot.

He indeed was foreordained before the foundation of the world, but was manifest in these last times for you who through Him believe in God, who raised Him from the dead and gave Him glory, so that your faith and hope are in God" I Peter 1:18-21.

We should never allow sin to come between ourselves and God. He wants us to bring it before Him, confess it, and move on. Sin impedes God's plan for our lives—whether a sin of the flesh, an attitude, a habit—whatever form it takes. We cannot expect to be Pacesetters for God if we can't approach Him because our own lives are in disorder. Notice the result of God's cleansing in Isaiah's life:

> *"Also I heard the voice of the Lord, saying: 'Whom shall I send, and who will go for Us?' Then I said, 'Here am I! Send me'"* Isaiah 6:8.

Two conditions change in Isaiah after he is cleansed by the Lord which become our fourth and fifth principle:

4. Cleansing invites *confidence* to serve God.

Have you ever noticed that when your relationship with the Lord is fresh and clean that you feel you are able to accomplish anything He asks of you? Isaiah immediately volunteers to fulfill the mission of God.

5. Cleansing is followed by *commissioning*.

God cannot use an unclean vessel. But when our lives are clean before Him, we have a greater sense of destiny and purpose. We know that He is with us, and that we can move out by His Spirit.

Today God is calling out a similar question: *Whom shall I send? He* is looking for men and women who will carry His standard of righteousness to the nations, one person at a time, city by city, country by country. Have you heard His call? Notice that Isaiah could not hear the voice of God until he was clean, and God does not hear us when we are unclean, either! Psalm 66:18 says, *"If I regard iniquity in my heart, the Lord will not hear me."* *(NIV)* Being clean before God is necessary for two-way communication!

God is calling this generation to become Pacesetters and bring His message of hope to a world without hope. Paul asked how people would ever hear the gospel if nobody bothered to evangelize. Isaiah responded to the call of God saying, "Here am I. Send me!" The commission to which Isaiah was assigned is the same one assigned to you and me and every other Christian: Go and tell the people the Good News about Jesus Christ. It's called the Great Commission and it is a command, not a suggestion:

> *"Go therefore and make disciples of all the nations, baptizing them in the name of the Father, Son and of the Holy Spirit, teaching them to observe all that I have commanded you; and lo, I am with you always, even to the end of the age"*
> Matthew 28:19-20.

Even after He commissions us, God promises that His presence will go with us. We must respond to the command of God and go forth in His name. How fitting that the very presence which **convicted** us of our sins, brought us to **confession**, **cleansed** us, gave us **confidence** in our task, and **commissioned** us in our ministry, would also accompany us on our assignments for Him, even until the end of the age!

---

1. Samuel Brengle, as quoted by J. Oswald Sanders, <u>Spiritual Leadership</u>, (Chicago: Moody Press, 1994), p. 19
2. Jerry Bridges, <u>The Pursuit of Holiness</u>, (Colorado Springs: NavPress, 1980), p. 27-28.
3. Billy Graham, <u>Unto the Hills</u>, (Waco, Word Books, 1986), p. 75.

Chapter Seven

Uzziah: Great Start, Weak Finish

> "If anyone would like to acquire humility, I can, I think, tell him the first step. The first step is to realize one is proud. And a biggish step, too. At least, nothing whatever can be done before it. If you think you are not conceited, you are very conceited indeed."[1]
>
> From "Mere Christianity" by C. S. Lewis

In a previous chapter, I discussed the importance of running to win. If we are to be Pacesetters we must run with a determination to see the finish line. We learned that David was a man who stayed in the fight until it was over; and Isaiah saw the process of repentance and commissioning through to completion. But you and I know that some who are called to a task never experience a satisfactory conclusion. In this chapter I'm going to discuss ways to guard against weak finishes. We are going to take a look at a man who started off with tremendous potential as a Pacesetter, only to wind up humiliated and broken: Uzziah, King of Judah.

Though all of us are equal in the eyes of the Lord as He enables us, not all of us compete as we should. Why do some of the most brilliant beginnings fizzle out in frustration? Why are some of the greatest ministries dashed to the ground in pieces as the enemy gloats? I believe the answer is rooted in the foundation of all sin: **PRIDE**. Of all the sinful conditions of the heart which beset us, it is pride that will bring down the best-intentioned Pacesetter if it is not dealt with in a serious and weary manner. The late scholar-writer, C.S. Lewis, asserts that pride is the "essential vice, the utmost evil." He goes on to say:

> *"Unchastity, anger, greed, drunkenness, and all that are mere flea bites in comparison: it was through pride that the devil became the devil: Pride leads to every other vice: it is the complete anti-God state of mind."*[2]

If pride is "the complete anti-God state of mind," as Lewis puts it, then the only way to enjoy a successful conclusion to a God-called task is to carry it out in a God-led attitude of humility and dependability. Zig Ziglar is one of America's greatest motivational speakers. In his highly-acclaimed book, *See You At the Top,* he makes a simple but compelling statement: "Ability is important—dependability is critical."[3] Yes, it is important that we recognize the God-given abilities we possess, but we must remember that they are, in fact, *God-given* and to be used for His glory and at His disposal. We must be able *and* dependable! With God's help we can be both!

Uzziah's Great Start

The story we are going to read takes place in the book of Second Chronicles. The four historical books (I and II Kings, and I and II Chronicles) give us a wealth of information concerning God's dealings with His people before their destruction. They are worth reading because they contain a great lesson on not learning a lesson! Read with me:

> *"Now all the people of Judah took Uzziah, who was sixteen years old, and made him king instead of his father Amaziah.*
> *He built Elath and restored it to Judah, after the king rested with his fathers.*
> *Uzziah was sixteen years old when he became king, and he reigned fifty-two years in Jerusalem. His mother's name was Jecholiah of Jerusalem"*
> II Chronicles 26:1-3.

What a great start for any Pacesetter! Here is a sixteen year old boy, a teenager, who has been proclaimed by popular demand to be king over the nation. You can imagine the pressure he was under from court officials from the previous reign, as well as family members and others who wondered if this "kid" had the goods to be king. I'm sure this was some of the pressure that young Timothy was feeling when he became the pastor in Ephesus. But listen to Paul's words of encouragement to his disciple and fellow minister:

> *"Let no one despise your youth, but be an example to the believers in word, in conduct, in love, in spirit, in faith, in purity"* I Timothy 4:12.

God is not limited by age or lack of experience; He is only limited by us when we don't allow Him full access to our lives.

Young Uzziah demonstrated wisdom from the very beginning. The text tells us two essential elements for a Pacesetter's success:

1. **Uzziah did what was right in the eyes of the Lord.**
2. **He sought out men of God like the prophet Zechariah.**

The Bible tells us that when we surround ourselves with wicked influences, we will be compromised. But if we seek out godly counsel and humbly accept it, we will honor the Lord in all we do. Uzziah chose to do things God's way. The result was outstanding:

> *"Now he went out and made war against the Philistines, and broke down the wall of Gath, the wall of Jabneh, and the wall of Ashdod; and he built cities around Ashdod and among the Philistines.*
> *God helped him against the Philistines, against the Arabians who lived in Gur Baal, and against the Meunites"* II Chronicles 26:6-7.

The Lord was with Uzziah and executed vengeance upon the traditional enemies of Judah: the Philistines and the Ammonites. The nation of Judah seemed unstoppable: Uzziah reorganized the army, supplied his men with new weapons, innovated novel military tactics and grew in power and reputation throughout the region. The lesson for us is simple but significant: **If you do things God's way you will have success! Victory is the natural result of obedience to God.** The enemy stands no chance against a person who is completely sold out to the Lord, provided that the man or woman of God remembers from whence cometh his or her strength. This is where the story turns for the Pacesetter king.

The Scripture indicates that another battle was being waged from within Uzziah's heart; pride was taking over.

"But when he was strong his heart was lifted up, to his destruction..." II Chronicles 26:16.

Pride is one of those subtle sins which can overtake a person by inches. I believe this is how it has always been for everyone who has been destroyed by pride, from Lucifer who would have exalted himself over the Most High to you and me. Most people do not start out with the intention of self-destructing. But the reason most people self-destruct is rooted in pride. Why is pride so bad? Isn't it good to be proud of some things?

Of course. There is a healthy pride which all of us need in order to be motivated and enjoy a positive self-esteem. When pride is anchored in God's perspective, it is a wonderful attitude:

—**the pride of new parents as the miracle of birth brings them a child,**

—**the pride of a little-league coach as his team loses gracefully,**

—**the pride of a wife as she watches her husband read to his children,**

—**the pride of our Heavenly Father as He watches us mature.**

These types of pride are to be exercised and nourished because they are dependent upon a relationship which is healthy and affirming. Pride which is centered in God and our relationship to Him is essential.

However, there is a pride which is rooted in self. This is the pride which nourishes rebellion, destruction, selfishness and independence. This pride is the "anti-God" attitude C.S. Lewis described. This is the pride which brought down Lucifer and turned him into Satan. It is what led Adam and Eve to disobey God and lose Paradise; which caused men to build a tower at Babel; which brought down Samson and Solomon; which caused Jonah to become embittered and Judas to become a traitor. Pride has seen the destruction of great nations, great ministries and great people.

Proverbs 16:18 says, *"Pride goes before destruction, a haughty spirit before a fall."* A self-sufficient attitude sets us up for a collapse, and this certainly was the case in Uzziah's life. When pride entered into the picture he started doing things his way instead of God's way. You can imagine the result, but let's read about it instead:

> *"...for he transgressed against the Lord his God by entering the temple of the Lord to burn incense on the altar of incense"* II Chronicles 26:16.

This may not sound like any tremendous sin to us, burning a little incense. He was doing it to honor the Lord, wasn't he? The problem was not the incense. The problem was the methodology. **God is very interested in things being done His way. The little things *DO* matter.** Remember how King Saul got into trouble for not following Samuel's instructions to the letter? His flippancy cost him his kingdom and ultimately his life.

> *"So Azariah the priest went in after him, and with him were eighty priests of the Lord—valiant men.*
> *And they withstood King Uzziah, and said to him, 'It is not for you, Uzziah, to burn incense to the Lord, but for the priests, the sons of Aaron, who are consecrated to burn incense. Get out of the sanctuary, for you have trespassed! You shall have no honor from the Lord God'"* II Chronicles 26:17-18.

What a demonstration of the grace and patience of our Lord! Notice what is happening here; God is giving Uzziah the chance to back out of his plan. The priests are a "red flag" of the Lord telling him to stop this behavior before it is too late. And this is the danger of pride. Pride overrides and hardens our hearts to the point of willful disobedience to God. Pharaoh might have saved himself a lot of trouble had he relented and let the people go a few plagues earlier, but his pride would not allow him that "disgrace." Rather, he continued on in his duel with God and paid a heavy price.

We must be sensitive to the "red flags" God sends our way. Sometimes they come in the form of people; other times they are a circumstance; but the proven way to perceive a stop signal from the Lord is by reading His Word and listening to the Holy Spirit's counsel. The Word tells us how we should behave quite clearly, while the Holy Spirit compels us to continue in the truth and attempts to steer us from those disobedient paths onto which we stray. *Proverbs 16:25 says, "There is a way that seems right to a man, but in the end it leads to death."* God help us to hear his voice and avoid those things which "seem" right at the time.

This principle is so evident as I decided to move to Washington. The Lord had opened up the door for a new ministry and I decided to take the position. After I had taken the new position I had a horrible fear that I had made the wrong decision. I began to contemplate how I was going to ask for my old position back. Then I asked the Lord if I made the right decision and He answered me by the Holy Spirit, the Word (God has not given us the Spirit of Fear) and by a confirmation by another dear brother in the Lord. God helped me avoid what seemed right at the time, and kept me on the road to Washington. Because I listened to His voice I have seen God explode the ministry.

The Price of Pride

"Then Uzziah became furious; and he had a censer in his hand to burn incense. And while he was angry with the priests, leprosy broke out on his forehead, before the priests in the house of the Lord, beside the incense altar.

And Azariah the chief priest and all the priests looked at him, and there, on his forehead, he was leprous; so they thrust him out of that place. Indeed he also hurried to get out, because the Lord had struck him" II Chronicles 26:19-20.

Uzziah's pride manifested itself in rage. The king became angry with God's extension of grace which the priests were offering (by trying to make him change his mind). Anger and rage are a common result of pride which has been assailed by righteousness. Why? Because pride is an unruly stallion which resists being tamed. Darkness does not understand light, and sin does not enjoy being exposed, especially pride. Uzziah lost control and pride drove him to stubborn disobedience.

The result: God must judge the unrepented sin of everyone, from a king to a bum. Notice that Uzziah never actually committed the sin of firing up the incense. But his attitude reflected the condition of his heart so that the event itself became a side issue. This is what Jesus is talking about when He says that to even hate a brother in one's heart is to commit murder; or to lust after a woman in one's heart is to commit adultery with her (see Matthew 5:21-30). Whether or not the murder or adultery actually occurs, the person harboring those thoughts is held responsible just as if the event happened.

Uzziah opened the Pandora's Box of pride and the resulting sin carried with it the heavy price of judgment. It's interesting that the Lord chose leprosy as the affliction of the king. The first action of the priests was to usher Uzziah out of the holy temple before he further profaned it. Why? Because leprosy carried with it several stigmas which Jewish society recognized.

The old Levitical laws declared that leprosy was an unclean condition requiring immediate attention as well as quarantine outside of society. Only the priests could declare a person clean after a bout with leprosy, and then only after following the prescribed treatment. In the meantime, the poor soul who was leprous was made to walk around shouting, "Unclean! Unclean!" wherever he or she went.

Accordingly, the rite of purification administered meticulously by the priests resolved itself in two parts: (1) The re-admission of the sufferer (Leviticus 14:1-9), who had been looked upon as dead, into the society of the living, and preparation for his return to fellowship with the covenant people, and (2) actual admission to the camp.[4] More symbolically, however, was the connection of Uzziah's sin with leprosy:

1. Leprosy was a visible disease which slowly ate away at the body. Just as Uzziah's pride slowly crept up on him as he grew in power, so would this disease slowly overtake him— a reminder for the rest of his life of the price of prideful disobedience.

2. Leprosy, like sin, made a person unclean. The Levitical considerations aside, leprosy had a social stigma attached to it, not unlike AIDS and other sexually transmitted diseases of our day. Just as in AIDS, a person may carry the virus for years before it begins to outwardly effect a person, so it is with the sin which we think we are hiding. Eventually it is going to find its way out.

3. Leprosy, like sin, isolates a person. As I said earlier, the priests would quarantine a person with leprosy outside the camp until the disease abated. Our sin separates us from the Lord and keeps us from fellowship with other believers until we are declared clean by Him. Once clean, it is as if we have returned from the dead and resumed our lives again with the covenant people.

4. Leprosy, like sin, can only be dealt with God's way. The priests faithfully followed God's treatment for leprosy. If they veered away from the prescribed instructions, they were guilty of disobedience. In the same way, there is only one recourse for us when we are unclean because of sin— the blood of Jesus applied by our faith and repentance. There is no other way to deal with our guilty past except through God's plan of redemption via Calvary.

Uzziah's Weak Finish

For the remainder of his life (some 10 years) Uzziah remained in isolation in a separate house from the palace. He was never again allowed access to the temple of the Lord, and his son Jotham ruled in his place, first as regent and after Uzziah's death, as king. The tremendous beginning of a sixteen year old who sought after the Lord ended in humility and loneliness.

Lest we judge Uzziah too harshly, it would be wise to understand that all of us are susceptible to the subtle lure of pride. Pacesetters must always operate in humility and recognize the danger signs of a prideful attitude. Thank God for His "red flags!" Keep them coming, Lord!

1. C.S. Lewis, The Joyful Christian, 127 Readings from C. S. Lewis, as quoted from his book Mere Christianity, (New York: Macmillan Publishing Company, 1977), p.141.
2. Ibid, p. 164.
3. Zig Ziglar, See You at the Top, (Gretna, Louisiana: Pelican Publishing Company, 1975), p. 24.
4. Merrill Unger, Unger's Bible Dictionary, (Chicago: Moody Press, 1971), p. 654.

Chapter Eight

Beware of
the Boat!

> *"You have a destiny to fulfill. You're the only one who
> can do it. Nothing is more fulfilling personally. And
> nothing makes a greater impact on the world around
> you."* [1]
>
> From "Victory: The Principles of
> Championship Living" by A.C. Green

Take the following test:

1. I consider myself a normal person.   YES ___ NO ___
2. I consider myself a normal Christian.   YES ___ NO ___
3. I consider myself an abnormal person.   YES ___ NO ___
4. I consider myself an abnormal Christian. YES ___ NO ___

SCORE: If you answered YES to questions three and four,
you are well on the way to a successful Christian life filled

with adventure and accomplishment. If you answered YES to questions one and two, you're in the same boat as 90% of the Christian and non-Christian world who are "normal." If you answered YES to all four questions you and your other personality need to come to some agreement (not to mention some counseling).

The point? Simple really. God is not impressed with the norm, but is looking for the abnormal in His people. No, I don't mean God is looking for people with two heads. **Abnormal means out of the ordinary; beyond the normal; out of place; separate from the rest.** God is interested in people willing to be different because to live the life of faith requires that we be different. Paul said he didn't mind being labeled a "fool for Christ" if that was what it took for some to be saved. Jesus called us salt and light to *distinguish* us from the rest of the world, not to compare ourselves with it. By the way, the eccentric people in the world, those who are considered a little strange or abnormal, often accomplish wonderful feats: Thomas Edison, Ben Franklin, Albert Einstein, Wolfgang Mozart—these (and countless others) have been considered strange by their contemporaries, yet today they are recognized as men of innovation and genius.

Consider the bizarre behavior of some of God's prophets. What must the Jews have thought of Ezekiel laying naked first on one side, and then the other, for days on end? How do you think they felt about Jeremiah railing at them in the Temple? Jesus was judged strange by His own family, who wanted to take Him home so they could keep an eye on Him. So, who wants to be an ordinary Christian when they can be an extraordinary one?

—Ordinary Christians are afraid of giants; *extraordinary Christians kill them.*

—Ordinary Christians seldom forget; *extraordinary Christians always forgive.*

—Ordinary Christians fight for their rights; *extraordinary Christians have no rights.*

—Ordinary Christians fear death; *extraordinary Christians have already died.*

In case you haven't surmised this yet, I see little qualitative difference between a normal Christian and a normal non-Christian apart from a religious bent on the part of those claiming to be Christians. Otherwise, the church today is fairly watered down with mediocre believers who statistically differ very little from the unbelieving world in every moral category, including divorce. If that's normal, you can keep it!

Watchman Nee, the Chinese Christian who lived earlier in this century, wrote a wonderful book called *The Normal Christian Life.* The thesis of this classic book on living for Christ is that Christians should so inhabit the supernatural that the supernatural comes naturally to us. In other words, the supernatural becomes the normal way of life for Christians. We should experience the extraordinary as an ordinary experience.

In *Authentic Christianity*, Ray Stedman suggests the difference between what he calls "the real thing" and imitation is found in what is being produced:

> *"There are five unmistakable signs of genuine Christianity: unquenchable optimism, unvarying success, unforgettable impact, unimpeachable integrity, and undeniable reality. They are always present whenever the real thing is being manifested. Mere religion tries to imitate these marks, but is never quite able to pull it off. By comparison with these marks, phony Christianity is always shown up to be what it is—a shabby, shoddy imitation that quickly folds when the real pressure is on...It is not being a Christian which produces (the real thing), but living as a Christian."[2]*

Unfortunately the church today has it backwards. We want the power without paying the price; we want the faith without stepping out of the boat. Instead of supernatural manifestations being the norm, they are a novelty. Whenever people hear about God moving miraculously in a service somewhere in the country, they want to get to that meeting in that city "where God is moving," and they browbeat their pastor wondering why God is not moving in their church! My question is, why should we have to travel across the country to see God manifest His power when He is more than willing to show His power within our own churches if given half a chance? Is God more powerful in Dallas than Des Moines?

But before that happens God must be given access to the local church. I'm sure it wasn't the building, or the great preaching, or the friendly people which attracted God to a little church on Azusa Street in Los Angeles at the beginning of the century to pour out a new Pentecost. It was a group of people who were hungry for God and willing to pay the price of faith and prayer and ridicule which brought the Holy Spirit in such powerful fashion. The same Spirit who poured Himself out on Azusa Street is available to any people who will give Him entrance into their hearts and churches.

I believe God wants to bring the church to a place where the supernatural becomes the norm; where Christians are not afraid to dream about and reach for the impossible; where people will be willing to take risks for the kingdom of God; where believers will be willing to do the ridiculous in order to see the miraculous. Would-be Pacesetters need to get out of the boat of comfortable Christianity and take some risks for the sake of Christ.

It reminds me of a young man named Brian Tate. Brian was a hard core party animal for the devil. One day Brian came to one of my meetings and got saved...he was radically touched by the Holy Spirit. Brian was a man who did not want to be ordinary, but wanted to take some risks for the Lord. He would often tell me how crazy he was living for the devil, so he wanted to be more radical for God. Brian was a man who took risks for God as he would go out into the streets and witness to anything that moved. Often times we would go into a burger place and Brian would get out of the car and begin witnessing for the Lord. He has never wanted to be in the boat of "comfortable" Christianity. Since then this young man has ministered in New Orleans during Mardi Gras...preached on the streets of Phoenix, and has worked inner city bus ministry. He has stepped out of the boat to be a *Pacesetter*.

Let's take a page from the apostle Peter's life and see how he moved from passenger to Pacesetter. Peter is one of those guys who has kind of a checkered record. Church history has been a little unfair to Peter at times, remembering that he denied Christ but underplaying his sermon on the day of Pentecost. He's become the butt of jokes—the buffoonish apostle who made good. But Peter demonstrates something that all of us need to have working in our lives: innocent, child-like faith which will take a chance even at great personal expense.

The story we're dealing with picks up in the book of Matthew just after Jesus has heard of the death of His cousin, John the Baptist. Jesus must have been burdened by this news as He ministered to and fed some 15,000 people. After taking care of the crowd, Jesus goes off alone to pray.

"Immediately Jesus made His disciples get into the boat and go before him to the other side, while he sent the multitude away.
After he had sent the multitudes away, he went up on the mountain by Himself to pray..."
Matthew 14:22-23a.

What an example Jesus is for us! Here He is, the Son of God, going off by Himself to pray. The temptation to most of us after a hard day's ministry coupled with disheartening news would be to go home and collapse for a few days. The fact of John's death only underscored for Jesus the reality that His days, too, were numbered. Maybe that's why He felt the need to pray. Now it's been said many times before, but if Jesus, being Jesus, prayed with such intensity; how much more should we, who would be Pacesetters, feel the need for prayer. In fact, this introduces a key principle: *Prayer and communion with God are essential for being a Pacesetter.* It is in the quiet moments with God that Jesus regains His strength. If you are not spending regular time with the Lord in prayer and communion, your effectiveness for Him is severely limited. We can't set the pace if we're not in the race. It is essential that we have a disciplined prayer life.

Notice also that Jesus gave the disciples a purpose, a definite order to get into the boat and go to the other side. The word used by Matthew is the Greek word "anankazo" which means to constrain, whether by threat, entreaty, force or persuasion. What was the hurry? John's gospel gives a little more light on the incident in John 6:15. Apparently, after feeding the people, the crowd was trying to force Jesus to become their king. He needed to get out of there, and fast! So he sent the men across the lake and he disappeared into the mountains to pray.

The point is that God will make His will known to us, either gently or if need be, by compelling us to go in a particular direction. Have you ever experienced an urgent indication by the Holy Spirit to pray for someone or to do something, even though you didn't understand at the time why you should? That is the compelling of the Holy Spirit which constrains us to obey God.

The Lord will not leave us hanging (for long) if we are truly seeking His direction in our lives. Sometimes it seems like an eternity before we get clear direction from the Lord, but we must allow for the mystery of God's perfect will and timing. Better to wait than to wish we had! Remember what the prophet Habakkuk experienced as he waited upon the Lord? God told him not to worry, that the answer was coming and would not delay, even though it seems to delay. There is a definite time-frame which God deals with and we must allow its full expression if we are going to experience God's perfect will in our lives.

Into the Boat

The disciples seated themselves in the little boat. These men knew each other very well: they slept, ate, ministered and traveled as a group. They were probably reasonably secure in their relationship with each other and with Jesus. They had developed a bond of security with each other; they were all in the same boat both literally and figuratively.

Alas, the boat can become a snare, if we allow it to create a clannish or exclusive attitude. It's natural to feel safety around people we know; the boat feels good! But we must beware of the boat! There's an old saying that there is "safety in numbers." How true! Humans feel much more secure around other humans. In times of great catastrophe even the bitterest enemies will become allies. This communal security blanket can be detrimental, however, to an organization like a church, whose function is to continue enveloping new people. Why? Because church people often find themselves afraid of stepping out or making changes which might attract more parishioners because they are afraid that their security will somehow be compromised; "it just won't be the same." What a selfish attitude! We must be willing to include people in our fellowship in an ever-widening circle of friendship and ministry or risk being reclusive, stagnant and ultimately alone.

"Now when evening came, He was alone there. But the boat was now in the middle of the sea, tossed by the waves, for the wind was contrary"
Matthew 14: 23b-24.

As the disciples attempted their crossing, the water pounded their little boat. Now, they were following Jesus' instructions to cross over, yet they were experiencing difficulty in the process. You mean sometimes when we are attempting something for God we will experience difficulties? Yes! Another principle here: **Pacesetters will experience problems.**

We would be unwise to believe that everything will go our way just because we are working for the Lord. In fact, we should anticipate struggles as a part of the honor in serving God. The same Peter whom we are dealing with in this chapter wrote in his first epistle:

"Beloved, do not think it strange concerning the fiery trial which is to try you, as though some strange thing happened to you; but rejoice to the extent that you partake of Christ's sufferings, that when His glory is revealed, you may also be glad with exceeding joy"
I Peter 4:12-13.

Peter is telling us that a normal part of the Christian life is the pain that sometimes accompanies it. But it is a glorious, shared suffering we participate in with our Lord. We are to rejoice in our trials, and to expect them!

When I was crossing the English Channel a few years ago, I boarded one of the numerous ferries that make daily crossings and had an uneventful trip from England to the

Continent. Just a few weeks earlier the same ferry system I was on experienced a disaster as one of the boats capsized in the Channel with much loss of life. One never knows when the unexpected will overtake us:

—Loss of a loved one,

—A bad report from medical tests,

—A betrayal from a trusted friend.

But...we know that God is greater than our disasters and He will see us safely from port to port.

One of the greatest tricks of the enemy is to make us feel pressure from our friends, real or otherwise. The devil loves to whisper in our ear that we are becoming "too radical"; "Nobody likes a religious nut"; and other not-so-sweet-nothings in an effort to make us behave more "normally." But you and I know that God has called us to live beyond the normal. We are Pacesetters, not trend followers! Remember the old saying: **You cannot make an impact without a collision.** Are you willing to collide for Christ?

No Boat? No Problem!

"Now in the fourth watch of the night Jesus went to them, walking on the sea.

And when the disciples see Him walking on the sea, they were troubled, saying, 'It is a ghost!' And they cried out for fear" Matthew 14:25-26.

Jesus had a challenge which would be quite an obstacle for someone normal, but Jesus was anything but normal. You see, He wanted to join the disciples, but He had no boat. The disciples were still struggling against the waves to make it across the lake—by now it was 3:00 AM! But Jesus did what came naturally...He walked on the water to meet the boat.

You can imagine why the disciples were startled at Jesus' appearance. First of all, it was dark and the only light was whatever was naturally available to the men (stars, moon, etc.). Suddenly, they see a figure at a distance, on top of the water, heading straight for them. They know in their minds that nothing human walks on water—it just isn't natural. So they scream in fear. Mark's gospel adds a humorous element stating that Jesus not only approached the boat, but was passing it by (see Mark 6:48). The disciples were making such slow progress that Jesus was beating them walking! According to folklore, if a sailor saw a ghost it meant that the ship was doomed to some disastrous end. But then they realized it was Jesus:

> *"But Jesus immediately spoke to them, saying, 'Be of good cheer! It is I; do not be afraid!'"*
> Matthew 14:27.

What a calming effect our Savior has upon us! When trouble surrounds us we should look for Jesus' appearance. He promised never to leave or forsake us—and His plans for us are good! The prophet Jeremiah declared:

> *"For I know the thoughts that I think toward you, says the Lord, "thoughts of peace and not of evil, to give you a future and a hope."* Jeremiah 29:11.

God does not lead us out so far in order to set us up for calamity. He has a plan to carry through for His glory. Jesus never plans a disaster for us.

Peter Sets the Pace...and Wets His Face

> *"And Peter answered Him and said, 'Lord, if it is you, command me to come to You on the water.'*

So He said, 'Come.' And when Peter had come down out of the boat, he walked on the water to go to Jesus" Matthew 14:28-29.

In every crowd there are those who will watch the pace be set and those who will attempt to set the pace. Peter was a definite Pacesetter. He was not willing to sit in the boat with everybody else. He wanted to experience walking on water with Jesus—to bridge the impossible in order to be with his Lord. What are you doing to approach the Lord? What bridges must you cross in order to make the connection with Christ? Here is a list of minimums which all Pacesetters must do on a regular basis if we are to come to Jesus:

Pray
Worship
Study the Word
Fellowship with Christians

Oh yes...there is something else we must do as we approach Jesus. We must keep our eyes on Him:

"And when Peter had come down out of the boat, he walked on the water to go to Jesus.
But when he saw that the wind was boisterous, he was afraid; and beginning to sink he cried out, saying, 'Lord, save me!'" Matthew 14:29-30.

Remember in an earlier chapter I said that fear is a paralyzer? Peter was completely disabled because he allowed the fear of his circumstances to overcome his faith. The result was that he lost his focus of Jesus and looked to the situation. Now you and I know that it is impossible to walk on water in the first place, and if on top of that realization, you remove the faith element, you're going to get wet. Another principle at work: *Pacesetters keep their eyes on Jesus—especially during the tough times*. The problem with Peter is that be began to look at all the things that were happening around him. The waves and the wind were always a factor that Peter had to face. The nagging fear of trying something that never had been done was facing Peter. However, Peter focused in on Jesus who is the author and finisher of our faith. At first, Peter was realizing that he was more than a conqueror, an overcomer over the circumstances of life, and then Peter took his eyes off of Jesus. If we take our eyes off the Lord, we are going to sink.

Peter's response is to cry out to the Lord for help, and Jesus graciously responds, though He adds a rebuke:

> *"And immediately Jesus stretched out His hand and caught him, and said to him, 'O you of little faith, why did you doubt?'*
> *And when they got into the boat, the wind ceased.*
> *Then those who were in the boat came and worshipped Him, saying, 'Truly You are the Son of God'"*
> Matthew 14:31-33.

William Barclay's commentary on Matthew presents us with three things typifying Peter's relationship with the Lord:

1. Peter was given to acting upon impulse and without thought of what he was doing. We know this is true elsewhere in Scripture. But Peter's intentions were always good ones.

2. Because Peter acted on impulse he often failed and came to grief. Several times Jesus had to reprimand Peter for brash statements or unwise actions.

3. Ultimately, Peter never failed because he always managed to clutch at Christ. Peter learned that to fail is not to sin; but to give up is a great sin. He always managed to finish with Jesus.[3]

We can be assured that as we approach Jesus, He will be faithful to guide and keep us every step of the way. Psalm 40 is a beautiful portrait of the Lord's willingness to guard and preserve us. Let's read a portion:

> *"I waited patiently for the Lord; and He inclined to me, and heard my cry.*
>
> *He also brought me up out of a horrible pit, out of the miry clay, and set my feet upon a rock, and established my steps.*
>
> *He has put a new song in my mouth—Praise to our God; many will see it and fear, and will trust in the Lord"* Psalm 40:1-3.

When the disciples in the boat witnessed the experience of Peter they did exactly what the psalmist describes: *they put their trust in the Lord* and reaffirmed His divinity. Jesus was concerned with a larger issue than being acclaimed Son of God by the disciples. He put the hard question to Peter about his faith even as He was saving him. I sometimes wonder if He did this privately or within earshot of the others. *Why did you doubt?*, Jesus asked Peter. Has He asked this of you recently?

A Commendation

We need to recognize something about Peter before we are too hard on him. *He got out of the boat!* Peter might not have had perfect faith and he might have been a person of impulse, but he had faith enough to get things started when everyone else was willing to wait. He set the pace for the others who saw the whole thing and they were encouraged by the episode even if he did sink. I'd, like Peter, **rather be a wet water walker than a dry boat talker!** Pacesetters don't lose by failing, they lose by quitting. We must persevere in our faith regardless of past failures or fears.

Pacesetter, God is looking for people in whom He can invest Himself. Are you a good risk? A wise investor will only risk his money when he is reasonably sure of a profitable return. Are you worthy of the Lord's investment? Unless you are willing to take a risk, you are not a good risk. God is looking for:

—**People who will dare the impossible,**
—**People who will walk on water if necessary,**
—**People who He can lift up and encourage in their faith.**

Let Him lift you up today...and by the way, if you're a little bit wet, you're in excellent company!

---

1. A.C. Green, <u>Victory: The Principles of Championship Living</u>, (Orlando: Creation House, 1994), p. 88.
2. Ray Stedman, <u>Authentic Christianity</u>, (Portland: Multnomah Press, 1975), p. 33.
3. William Barclay, <u>The Gospel of Matthew, Vol. 2,</u> (Philadelphia: The Westminister Press, 1975), p. 106-107.

Chapter Nine

People of Passion

> *"No heart of a child of God will ever be satisfied with any object or person short of the Lord Jesus Christ."*[1]
>
> From the writings of Charles Spurgeon

In his memoirs, Charles Finney, the great evangelist of the last century, described his determination to obtain the passion of God in his life. God had been dealing with him and he decided that it was time either to accept God or "die in the attempt." He found his way to a clearing in the woods near his law office in Adams, New York, to a place where the trees formed a natural altar. He began to pray. Finney wrestled in prayer as he recounted past sins and failures in his life. The hours went by until, "all sense of sin, all consciousness of present sin or guilt had departed from me." Peace had finally come to Charles Finney.

Finney returned to the law office. It was now dusk and everyone had departed for the day. But the Holy Spirit was not finished yet and drove Finney to a back room to continue in prayer. Listen to Finney recount the wonderful experience he had as he moved to the back room in the office:

"There was no light in the room; nevertheless it appeared to me as it were perfectly light. As I went in and shut the door it seemed as if I met the Lord Jesus face to face—as I would see any other man. He said nothing, but looked at me in such a manner as to break me right down at His feet. It seemed to me a reality that He stood before me and I fell down at His feet and poured my soul out to Him. I wept like a child and bathed His feet with my tears."[2]

After the encounter with Jesus, Finney went into the next room and sat by the fire, thinking on the vision of Christ, when:

"...I received a mighty baptism by the Holy Ghost. Without expecting it the Holy Spirit descended upon me in a manner that seemed to go through my body and soul. I could feel the impression like a wave of electricity going through me. Indeed it seemed to come in waves and waves of liquid love...like the very breath of God...These waves came over me and over me until I recollect I cried out, "I shall die if these waves continue to pass over me...Lord I cannot bear anymore."[3]

You can understand why Finney's life was never the same after this tremendous encounter with Jesus. He eventually gave up his law career to become a preacher of the gospel. His revivals in up-state New York became world famous. Finney had a passion for God which was unquenchable—and it stemmed from a personal encounter with Jesus.

God is looking for people of passion. People who, like Finney, are willing to find an altar in the woods, or in their homes, or wherever they can be alone with God and pray until the answer comes. **He is looking for people who hunger and thirst after righteousness, and will not be satisfied until they have been filled; people who desire God more than anything else.**

What is passion? It is an intensely emotional or compelling attitude or feeling which calls people to action; a strong affection or love; a strong enthusiasm or desire; a violent anger. Passion evokes images of ardor, zeal and fervor. When James says that the *"effective and fervent prayer of a righteous man can accomplish much (James 5:16)"*, he is speaking of a fervent passion to pray.

Passionate Not Passive

We should seek for passionate Christianity, not passive Christianity. God has enough passive Christians with whom He must deal. But the passionate Christians are the ones who will accomplish great things for the kingdom. I just defined a passionate person. Now let's compare passion with passivity. To be passive means one is:

—enduring or submitting without resistance,
—inactive; not reacting visibly,
—being acted upon, rather than acting upon.

To be passive is not necessarily a bad thing. Obviously our attitude *toward* God must be passive, i.e., we submit to God without resistance, and allow Him to act upon us. But our attitude *for* God must be passionate. By being passionate we will be able to take on the gates of hell itself as God leads us from victory to victory.

Passionate people are powerful people. History shows us that nations have been moved by men and women of passion—for good or evil. In the right setting, passion can be a glorious motivator for positive change, such as Abraham Lincoln's attempts to end slavery and hold the Union together at all costs. In the wrong setting, however, passion can lead to disaster. Have you ever seen the old newsreels of Adolf Hitler giving a speech? The man might have been a monster, but he knew the art of passion to inflame a crowd and make them his willing subjects—and plunge the world into war.

Passion for God is more than an emotional experience, it is a relational one. It is an ever-present reality based upon our knowing Jesus. If passion was simply an emotional reaction to God, there would be down times when our passion would fizzle out. But we know that we can be completely drained of physical and spiritual strength yet still have a passion for God based upon the truth of our relationship with Him. Passion is maintained by faith, not feelings.

The passion of God delivered to us by the Holy Spirit can give us the ability to accomplish tremendous things. Paul writes:

> *"For what man knows the things of a man except the spirit of the man which is in him? Even so no one knows the things of God except the Spirit of God.*
>
> *Now we have received, not the spirit of the world, but the Spirit who is from God, that we might know the things that have been freely given to us by God.*
>
> *These things we also speak, not in words which man's wisdom teaches but which the Holy Spirit teaches, comparing spiritual things with spiritual"*
> I Corinthians 2:11-13.

It is the Holy Spirit who knows the mind of God intimately enough to forward His will to us. The Spirit must lead us in passionate relationship with the Father so we can understand His spiritual truths and activate them here on earth. The Bible is rich with the stories of men and women who developed a passion for God which led them to do tremendous exploits:

—Joseph's passion for God allowed him to overcome the temptations of Potiphar's wife and be cast in prison rather than compromise.

—Daniel's passion for God led him to defy the king's decrees not to pray, even at the risk of his life.

—Stephen's passion for God gave him the courage to testify about the Lord to the Sanhedrin before he was dragged out and stoned.

Let's take a look at another person of passion and how he accomplished great things for God: King Saul.

Saul's story is found in the book of I Samuel. Taken as a whole, the life of Saul is a tragic picture of the results of disobedience to God. There are some wonderful moments, however, in the life of Saul which illustrate the importance, as well as the result, of having passion for God.

The road to kingship for Saul began rather ignobly. Saul was searching for his father's lost donkeys when he came to the town where Samuel the prophet was ministering. Saul decided that Samuel might be able to tell him where the animals were. In the meantime, the Lord had instructed Samuel to anoint this stranger king. Reluctantly, Saul accepted the kingship, though they had to dig him out of the baggage where he was hiding (I Samuel 10:20-23). Most of the people accepted Saul as king, though some had their doubts about him ("troublemakers" the Bible calls them).

Saul was certainly unproven, and he had little self-confidence. He wasn't even a good hider!

Fortunately, God has a way of putting us in situations requiring passion on our part so we can see Him move, and this is exactly what happens to Saul. God stirs up a cause worth fighting for in Saul. Let's pick up the text in I Samuel 11 and watch a passive man evolve into a man of passion:

> *"Then Nahash the Ammonite came up and encamped against Jabesh Gilead; and all the men of Jabesh said to Nahash, 'Make a covenant with us, and we will serve you.'*
>
> *And Nahash the Ammonite answered them, 'On this condition I will make a covenant with you, that I may put out all your right eyes, and bring reproach on all Israel.'*
>
> *Then the elders of Jabesh said to him, 'Hold off for seven days, that we may send messengers to all the terrritory of Israel. And then, if there is no one to save us, we will come out to you'"* I Samuel 11:1-3.

Bullies have always been around it seems, even in biblical times. A local ruler of the Ammonites decided to inflict himself upon the people of Jabesh Gilead, a little town near the Jordan River. The Ammonites were distant cousins of the Israelis (the result of an incestuous episode between Lot and his youngest daughter in Genesis 19). They were notorious hit-and-run fighters with little stomach for a real war. The fact that these nomadic raiders could penetrate fairly deeply into Israelite territory demonstrates the low ebb of the Jews at the close of the era of the Judges.

Nahash, the Ammonite leader, is a type of Satan, his name meaning "serpent." Like Satan, Nahash is brash, proud and willing to settle, as long as it is to his advantage. He is quite confident of his position or he wouldn't be making such bold demands, and he especially would not allow the elders the seven days grace they were requesting unless he felt sure of his position. He is bent on humiliating the people of God as well as taking spoils. The mutilation of the population would bring a reproach on the nation for their inability to rescue one of their own cities, signaling not only a defeat of Israel, but of their God.

The city of Jabesh Gilead was inhabited by a passive population who had no stomach for a fight and could not depend upon relief from elsewhere, so they decided that it was better to settle with the enemy than be destroyed by him. **Jabesh Gilead means "a dry place,"** an appropriate name for a city whose people are spiritually dry and passive.

When we become dried out and passive in our Christian walk, we are the most vulnerable to an attack by the enemy. It is in this instance that we would rather make a treaty with the enemy than to fight him. This is exactly the place where the people of Jabesh Gilead found themselves.

Dealing With Darkness

The first point I want to make in this section is that *the people of God approached the enemy about making a covenant first.* Of course he is willing to make a deal, especially with God's people. Remember that though he is powerful, Satan is also a being with limited resources. It costs him less to settle than to fight, so why not settle? In the case of Judas Iscariot, it only cost him 30 pieces of silver. A cheap price to pay for the Prince of Peace.

Charles H. Spurgeon, the great preacher of the last century said of the devil in one of his sermons, "He is more cunning than the wisest: How soon he entangled Solomon! He is stronger than the strongest: How fatally he overthrew Samson! Yes, and men after God's own heart, like David, have been led into most grievous sins by his seductions."[4]To enter into covenant with Satan is to place yourself under house arrest, you have freedom to move about, but you are imprisoned all the same.

When we become dry or passive in our relationship with God, we will begin to settle with the enemy, making deals and compromising our integrity until we are in servitude to him. We find ourselves saying things like:

> *"Aw, it's not so bad."*
> *"God will understand."*
> *"Hey, nobody is perfect!"*
> *"It's just a little thing!"*
> *"It's OK. God will forgive me."*

Lies, lies, lies. To enter into a deal with darkness is to buy into a lie. Once ground is given it becomes a narcotic to the enemy; he is never satisfied and will continue asking for more and more until he has everything. Believe me, Satan is a master of the old "you didn't read the fine print" ploy. That fine print has cost people their families, their jobs, even their lives. The poor people at Jabesh Gilead don't realize with whom they are dealing!

Let's Make a Deal

Just as we can only deal with the Lord on His terms, Satan will only come to terms with us if it is according to his plan. Nahash accepted the offer of a settlement, and immediately set the conditions of the covenant. If Satan senses that we are willing to settle he knows he has the advantage already and will begin upping the ante accordingly.

The demand in this case is the gouging out of everyone's right eye. There are a couple of reasons for this unusual stipulation:

First, this would bring disgrace on God's people because they were unable to prevent this from happening. Satan doesn't just want a win, he wants a humiliation of everything which stands for God. When he disgraces the people of God he brings reproach on the church and on God's credibility in the eyes of the world. Just think back to the black eye Christians took in the late 1980's during the televangelist disasters.

Second, disabling the people takes the fight out of them for future conflicts. Because most men held a shield in their left hand and a sword in their right when they fought the losing of their right eye would render them useless in a war; they couldn't see to fight! When the warrior would lift up his shield to defend against the enemy, the only eye he could see out of was his right eye. So, to gouge out the right eye would make a warrior powerless to strike back in an offensive manner. Therefore, there would be an army dressed up in all of their armor, but unable to inflict any damage to the enemy. The enemy wants to take the fight out of Christians by disabling us so that we won't be interested in a rematch. He'll attack us physically, emotionally, spiritually—however he can—until we become passive and therefore tamed.

A Cry for Help

The elders appeal to Nahash for seven days to seek help. These were men who could still remember the valiant men of old who did not compromise with the enemy. These elders had enough wisdom to ask for seven days (God's number of completion) to seek out help. Nahash agrees to this knowing that their is little, if any, chance that help will come in seven days. We must be alert to signals that passive people send out. Just because people have become passive, even to the point of numbness, does not mean that the spirit of

God cannot rekindle something of the old life in them. As God seeks to deliver people from their passive prisons, we must be the instruments to help and encourage them.

How can you tell when someone is in a passive prison? Here are some indicators. There are many, many more: Passive people:

—do not worship,
—neglect God's Word,
—are not careful about what they read or watch,
—do not attend church,
—are silent in their witness.

The text says that messengers were sent out across Israel to appeal for help. Who do you suppose they selected for the mission, men of passivity or men of passion? **I can guarantee that at a time like this men of passion were needed to carry the urgency of the message as to what was at stake.** I believe these were men who were probably married with many children. The reason being is that these men would continually have the vision of their wives and children having their right eye gouged out. This would spur these men on to get help because there was something at stake back in their city. There was a cause to be passionate about, and nothing was going to quench their passion to get help. These were men in Jabesh Gilead who had not succumbed to the dryness of life. These hand-picked men of passion were on a mission to save their friends and loved ones. Guess what? So are we.

"So the messengers came to Gibeah of Saul and told the news in the hearing of the people. And all the people lifted up their voices and wept.

Now there was Saul, coming behind the herd from the field; and Saul said, 'What troubles the people,

that they weep?' And they told him the words of the
men of Jabesh" I Samuel 11:4-5.

The message of the plight of their fellow Jews caused
the people to weep in compassion. Today I look at what is
happening to our own country, the United States, and I see
the passivity and the compromise; how the enemy has dealt
severely with us; how we have departed from our God; and it
makes me weep. Anyone who loves this country can see the
troubles we are in.

Yet, we must move beyond an emotional response and
get down to hard-core action if we are going to see this
country revived and God-centered once again. If there is
one thing which stirs Americans to unified action it is the
belief in a cause; it is a part of the American spirit woven
into the fabric of our nation from the very beginning. Christians must see the spiritual renewal of America as a cause
worth fighting for...just as Saul sees a cause in the Jabesh
situation:

> *"Then the Spirit of God came upon Saul when he*
> *heard this news, and his anger was greatly aroused"*
> I Samuel 11:6.

When Saul heard what the messengers had to say he was
furious. Suddenly the responsibilities of being king took on
a new meaning; here was a cause which was needful and
worthy of a fight. The Spirit of God came upon Saul as he
got mad at the devil. The enemy always looks smaller in the
eyes of faith and passion. **The key is this: a passion was
created in Saul by the Holy Spirit which stoked his faith
and set him on a course of action.** (By the way, the Spirit
never came upon a person to do a work without it being
successfully completed.) Pacesetters must develop an an-

131

ger against the works of darkness which will motivate them for action.

Passion Produces Action

"So he took a yoke of oxen and cut them in pieces, and sent them throughout all the territory of Israel by the hands of messengers, saying, 'Whoever does not go out with Saul and Samuel to battle, so it shall be done to his oxen.' And the fear of the Lord fell on the people, and they came out with one consent.

When he numbered them in Bezek, the children of Israel were three hundred thousand, and the men of Judah thirty thousand" I Samuel 11:7-8.

A call to arms went throughout the different tribes by way of a rather gruesome message: pieces of Saul's oxen. The point was clear: all of us are effected by this situation, so we must all fight or pay a heavy price. Paul's comparison of the Body of Christ to the human body and how all the parts must work together is a similar situation. When one part of the body hurts, it effects the whole. Saul was telling the people that if they did not come and help fight the battle, eventually the battle would come to them and nobody would help them. **The principle is apparent: Give and it shall be given unto you. Help someone else and you will be given help when you need it.**

This was also a critical test of Saul's new role as king. He was about to find out if his passion would move a nation to war. The results affirmed his leadership as well as the Lord's active participation in behalf of Saul. The fear of the Lord came upon them and helped convince them to fight.

The Enemy Scattered

Saul sent word to the elders at Jabesh that he would bring deliverance to them within a day. The people were elated and told the Ammonites that they would surrender the next day and would succumb to whatever they had in mind. This probably lulled the enemy into a false security, because that night Saul and his army attacked:

> *"So it was, on the next day, that Saul put the people in three companies; and they came into the midst of the camp in the morning watch, and killed Ammonites until the heat of the day. And it happened that those who survived were scattered, so that no two of them were left together"* I Samuel 11:11.

Nahash got more than he bargained for. He was anticipating a cheap victory and himself became passive. It cost him the battle. The enemy does not stand a chance against a people who are passionate for God. Pacesetters must realize that the Lord is calling us to do battle with the enemy, to release from captivity those who have been taken in by him, and to scatter the enemy and drive him out of the land. This can only be done through a passionate people with a passionate cause empowered by the Holy Spirit.

1. Charles Spurgeon, <u>2200 Quotations from the Writings of Charles H. Spurgeon,</u> compiled by Tom Carter, (Grand Rapids: Baker Books, 1988) p. 183.
2. Charles Finney, <u>The Autobiography oc Carles G. Finney,</u>edited by Helen Wessel. (Minneapolis, MN; Bethany House, 1977) p. 15
3. Ibid, p. 22
4. Spurgeon, p. 57.

Chapter Ten

Setting the Pace for Passion

> "God wants to make his ministers a flame of fire. Look at the change in discouraged, cringing, cowardly Peter; denying that he even knew Jesus. After the Holy Ghost was given, fire burned in his bones. The Holy Spirit of God opened up to him a new realm of faith, of courage and of power. If we are filled with that same Spirit, we should also be filled with that same confidence. And if we are filled with that same confident assurance of the early church, we should have the same courage and zeal of Peter and the other disciples." [1]
>
> From "Militant Evangelism" by Ray Comfort

Saul was a passive man who changed into a man of passion when he realized that there was a cause to fight for which was greater than himself. We too have a great cause, a modern-day crusade, for which we must fight:

—Our friends and families,
—Our communities,
—Our country,
—The next generation,
—Our own lives.

It is up to us who are Pacesetters to maintain a passion for the Lord that will allow us to minister with power and authority. The problem is that so many Christians are passive that they have forgotten what it was like to be passionate. How can we get the passion we need and keep it? Through relationship!

A passion for God is birthed out of a relationship with Him. I'm not talking about an emotional attachment, but a full-fledged relationship which motivates you to follow hard after God. The key to getting passion once the relationship has been established is to ask God to give you passion:

—Passion for the lost,
—Passion to live a pure life,
—Passion for His Word,
—Passion to pray,
—Passion to worship.

Maybe you have never had any real passion for God and so have never really experienced victory in these disciplines. Perhaps you once had a fiery passion for the Lord, but that passion has been drowned in a sea of passivity. Or possibly you have lost your way and desire to be restored to the Lord in a passionate relationship. Whatever the case, we're going to examine the life of a man who had a passion for God, lost it, and regained it: the prophet Elijah.

Elijah's Victory

During the days of King Ahab, God raised up a man named Elijah to minister in Israel. These were dark days for Israel as the people, encouraged by the king and a corrupted priesthood, worshipped the Baal gods and had forgotten the ways of the Living God. Elijah means "Jehovah is God," and he was a constant reminder that the God of Abraham was very much alive—even in a land being plunged deeper and deeper into pagan religion. A showdown between the God of Elijah and the god of the prophets of Baal was inevitable.

The day finally came for the encounter which occurred on Mt. Carmel. The Baalists tried every trick in the book to evoke their gods and get them to ignite the altar they had constructed. All day long they ranted, raved and cut themselves in an effort to draw out their god. Elijah watched the spectacle with an air of bemusement, offering a sarcastic comment every so often.

Finally Elijah decided it was his turn. He prayed to the Lord to ignite his altar of wood (though not before dousing it liberally with water to make sure the wood was nice and wet) and God responded beautifully. The demonstration of power by the Lord caused the people who had been watching to fall down in repentance and ask for forgiveness. Then the crowd, on Elijah's instruction, seized the prophets of Baal (numbering 450) and killed them all.

Elijah then proclaimed to King Ahab that the drought of the past three years was coming to an end and there would soon be rain. He warned the king that he had better get moving back to Jezreel if he wanted to make it before the rain might effect his ability to travel in his chariot. When the rain began, Elijah was so buoyed by the experience that he actually caught up with Ahab's chariot and passed him running on foot! What a tremendous day of victory for the Lord and Elijah! Yet, it was a short-lived victory as far as the enemy was concerned.

The Enemy Raises the Stakes

Let's pick up the story now from I Kings 19 and see what happens to Elijah after this marvelous defeat of the pagan prophets:

> *"And Ahab told Jezebel all that Elijah had done, also how he had executed all the prophets with the sword.*
>
> *Then Jezebel sent a messenger to Elijah, saying, 'So let the gods do to me, and more also, if I do not make your life as the life of one of them by tomorrow about this time.'*
>
> *And when he saw that, he arose and ran for his life, and went to Beersheba, which belongs to Judah, and left his servant there.*
>
> *But he himself went a day's journey into the wilderness, and came and sat down under a broom tree. And he prayed that he might die, and said, 'It is enough! Now, Lord, take my life, for I am no better than my fathers!'*
>
> *Then as he lay and slept under a broom tree, suddenly an angel touched him, and said to him, 'Arise and eat'"* I Kings 19:1-5.

Whenever there has been a victory for the forces of light, expect a violent reaction from the powers of darkness. It's kind of like throwing a rock at a beehive; the bees find it irritating and they fly around in a frenzy stinging anything in their way. So it was with Jezebel.

Jezebel was a patroness of the prophets of Baal. Her name according to some scholars is derived from the name Baal, as in Jeze-baal, "adoration of Baal." Other biblical linguists translate her name as "unchaste" and even "dunghill." Whatever her name meant, she was not the kind of woman you'd bring home to mother. She was infuriated at the humiliating defeat of her gods, especially since she was a foreigner who detested the God of Israel.

With the queen out for revenge, Elijah takes off. Notice the words of the queen: they are a proud boast and a fearsome threat. The devil specializes in boasts and threats because he can do more damage with intimidation than he can in an active engagement. Why? Because if he can intimidate us and force us out of the game, even for a while, he has greater resources to expend elsewhere. Intimidation costs the devil very little, although sometimes it costs us everything.

Elijah's Getaway

The enemy's poison worked its way into Elijah's heart and fear gripped him. The vow of Jezebel was too much for the man of God who had just faced down 450 prophets of Baal. The enemy has vowed to destroy us. It has always been his intention to bring down we who are made in the Father's image by whatever means necessary. It shouldn't surprise us then when from time to time he moves to fulfill that vow in our own life.

The lesson is simple: *Fear that is placed in our heart by the enemy will rob us of our passion for God.* Why is this? Because there is no room for fear and passion to cohabitate. Jesus said we can not serve two masters, so if we are serving fear we cannot be serving God; therefore, we cannot be passionate for God.

Elijah is so overcome with fear and personally disappointed with himself that he prays to God that he might die. Have you ever felt that way? We say something like, "Just let me die, Lord, and be with you!" Maybe you've never actually prayed to die, but you might have decided that it sure would be nice to go on into Glory. Guess what? That is a selfish attitude. Until God is ready to take you to be with Him, you must be prepared to continue serving Him. If the Lord took to heaven every Christian who has from time to time wanted to throw in the towel, there would be nobody left to preach the Gospel!

Paul even recognized the attractiveness of going to heaven versus staying on earth and enduring painful situations for the cause of Christ. He told the Philippians:

> *"For to me, to live is Christ, and to die is gain.*
> *But if I live on in the flesh, this will mean fruit from my labor; yet what I shall choose I cannot tell.*
> *For I am hard-pressed between the two, having a desire to depart and be with Christ, which is far better.*
> *Nevertheless to remain in the flesh is more needful for you"* Philippians 1:21-24.

He realized that the call of God goes beyond our personal comfort. We have a job to do, and to do fully. God is much more interested in what He is producing in our lives than He is in the personal distress it might cause from time to time. The reason is that He has promised to be with us during those difficult times, and He knows that He is producing both character in us and ministry to the world for Him. Paul realized something Elijah did not: *Your passion for God will diminish as you listen to the enemy.* We must learn to ignore the negative news of the devil and remain faithful and focused on the Word of God. If there is one thing which will stop the demonic in its tracks, it is truth. Light and darkness cannot abide in the same place. The light overcomes the darkness and exposes it for what it really is: a pack of lies. *When the enemy raises the stakes, we must raise the standard!*

Passion Regained

As Elijah slipped into sleep (what he thought was his final rest) the Lord was preparing to restore his confidence and faith. Thank God for His gracious attitude toward us that He will help us regain our passion for Him when we have spent ourselves. One of the Psalms describes the Lord as "inclining his ear toward us." In other words, God cares so much for us He will come down to our level and make Himself understood. This is what the Incarnation is all about: God becoming human so He can relate to us in an understandable way.

When Elijah awoke (though not in heaven as he had hoped) an angel ministered to him gave him something to eat. God was sustaining Elijah, feeding him so he might not only regain physical strength, but also to demonstrate that He was looking out for His prophet. *If we are going to have or regain a passion for God, we must eat at His table—* we must eat of the bread from heaven. There are three principles we can learn from this account as to how we can maintain or regain our passion for God:

1. We must eat the bread from heaven.

Jesus said, *"Man shall not live by bread alone, but by every word which proceeds out of the mouth of God."* We must not neglect taking care of our physical needs, but we must also take care of our spiritual needs. If we are not consuming the Word of God everyday, just like we eat a meal, then we will become weak in our passion for God. The road to restoration of passion for God begins with eating of the things of God, particularly of His Word.

The idea of bread symbolizing the Word is found throughout the Scriptures.

How like the Lord to use something as staple as bread as a spiritual illustration, since bread is found in one form or another in virtually every culture in the world. Let's look at the significance of the bread/word relationship in the Bible:

Genesis 14:18: Melchizidek, the king of Salem, brings out an offering of bread and wine for Abraham, symbol izing a pre-Christian body and blood communion experience.

Exodus 16:14: The Lord rains down "bread from heaven" for the people symbolizing His presence and His providence as He fulfills His Word to watch over His people.

Exodus 25:30: Instruction is given to the people about the Bread of the Presence in the tabernacle symbolizing God's dwelling with His people.

Then Jesus, who came not to abolish the Law of Moses but to fulfill it, that is give greater expression and understanding to it said:

> *"Then Jesus said to them, 'Most assuredly, I say to you, Moses did not give you the bread from heaven, but My Father gives you the true bread from heaven.*
>
> *For the bread of God is He who comes down from heaven and gives life to the world.'*
>
> *Then they said to Him, 'Lord, give us this bread always.'*
>
> *And Jesus said to them, 'I am the bread of life. He who comes to Me shall never hunger, and he who believes in Me shall never thirst'"* John 6:32-35.

If you have lost your passion, or are seeking it out for the first time, you will never discover it until you determine that you will feed daily from the Word of life. John describes Jesus as the "word become flesh." The implication is clear: if we are to truly have a living relationship with Jesus Christ, we must have a living relationship with His Word, because the two are inseparable. *You cannot keep the Word without Christ, and you cannot keep Christ without the Word.*

2. We must take time for physical rest and nourishment.

> *"Then he looked, and there by his head was a cake baked on coals, and a jar of water. So he ate and drank, and lay down again.*
> *And the angel of the Lord came back the second time, and touched him, and said, 'Arise and eat, because the journey is too great for you'"* I Kings 19:6-7.

I already discussed the importance of physical nourishment for our bodies. If we are going to maintain a vital passion for God, we must keep our bodies in good physical condition. What good is a passionate spirit if its vehicle is burning itself out? God knew that He was about to embark Elijah on a great journey and that his physical body needed restoration. As we'll see in a minute, even a little with God goes a long way.

Jesus understood this principle as well. Many times in the Scripture He would refresh Himself, and have His disciples do the same. If you desire to maintain or regain your passion for God, you have to take care of yourself. Remember, we are a temple of the Holy Spirit. We should treat our bodies as we do our churches—with respect and dignity.

There was a time when I was running, running and running. I found myself constantly doing things for the ministry. I was becoming tired because I was not practicing the principle of rest. One day an elder of my church came up to me and told me that I needed to take care of my body because it was the temple of God. He had noticed that I was getting a little haggard and that the solution was to spend some time relaxing. I found out that as I spent some time refeshing myself, that I was fit for the rest of the week. Remember, God spent six days creating and on the seventh— He rested!

3. We must go to the presence of God.

"So he arose, and ate and drank; and he went in the strength of that food forty days and nights as far as Horeb, the mountain of God" I Kings 19:8.

The Lord led Elijah on a 40-day trek through the wilderness to bring him to His presence at Mt. Horeb. Elijah was desperate for a breakthrough and probably would have followed the Lord to Mt. Everest if He had so called him. Why couldn't the Lord have simply appeared to Elijah where he was, instead of making him walk some 200 miles south? Several reasons:

A. The significance of the number 40. The number 40 in the Bible signifies a time of transition between events wherein the latter result involves a greater work of the Lord:
—It rained forty days and nights signifying the beginning and the end of God's wrath being poured out on the earth and a new beginning.
—Goliath taunted the armies of Israel 40 days before David killed him and began David's real rise to prominence in Israel.
—Jesus was tempted for 40 days and nights and overcame the devil before beginning his public ministry.

There are other examples of the number 40 playing a significant role in a transition in the Bible. The point is that Elijah's journey of 40 days allowed the Lord time to deal with the fears that Elijah was carrying. God knew that at the end of the journey, Elijah's passion would be restored and he would transit from a fearful man to a greater man of passion than ever before.

B. The significance of Mt. Horeb. It wasn't just any mountain to which God was bringing Elijah. Mt. Horeb was the mountain of God—the place where Moses had received the commandments after the exodus from Egypt; Mt. Horeb was also called Mt. Sinai! The Lord was teaching Elijah a spiritual illustration by bringing him to the very place where the nation of Israel began as a codified people. You can imagine the range of emotions that Elijah felt as he stood at the base of the very mountain Moses had climbed some six to seven hundred years earlier. Now Elijah was standing in the place of Moses, God's prophet to God's people. The Lord certainly knows how to drive home a point, doesn't He?

We must maintain a sense of urgency which will drive us to the presence of God. We must realize that we *are* standing in the place of Moses, Joshua, and Elijah, not to mention Jesus, to the same lost world they ministered to centuries ago. How urgent are you to be in the Lord's presence?

—We must be like the man on the pallet who had to get to Jesus even if it meant breaking through the roof to get to Him;

—We must be like the woman with the issue of blood who pressed through the crowds wanting merely to touch the Messiah;

—We must be like Mary, who sat at the feet of Jesus rather than doing what was seemingly more urgent in the kitchen.

If we are to be people of passion then we must do whatever it takes to stay in the presence of God. Like Elijah, we must pay whatever price and allow the Lord to minister His presence to us. His anointing resides in His presence; His healing is in His presence; His life is with Him. And as we draw near to Him, He promises to draw near to us. What a deal!

A Loaded Question

> *"And there he went into a cave, and spent the night in that place; and behold, the word of the Lord came to him, and He said to him, 'What are you doing here, Elijah?'"* I Kings 19:9.

In our moment of crisis it sometimes takes someone we love and who loves us to ask the hard questions and help us regain our perspective. God will often allow us to sink into depths of despair or self-pity before He intervenes. The reason for this is that until we come to the end of ourselves and realize that we do not have the answer, He can't really help us.

Throughout the Bible, God (or a person speaking for Him) makes the hard statements at moments of deep, personal crisis; kind of a "bolt from the blue" wake-up call :

Of Adam after the Fall, God asked, *"Who told you that you were naked?"*

Of Moses when he was afraid to speak before Pharaoh, God asked, *"Who has made man's mouth? Or who makes the mute, the deaf, the seeing, or the blind? Is it not I, the Lord?"*

Of Joshua who was despairing defeat at Ai, God said, *"Get up! Why do you lie on your face?"*

Of Saul, who had disobeyed Samuel's order to kill **all** the animals, Samuel asked, *"What is this bleating of the sheep* *in my ears, and the lowing of oxen which I hear?* (i.e. *What are these animals doing alive?*)

Of Jeremiah, when he was complaining about the difficulty of the ministry, God asked, *"If you have run with the footmen, and they have wearied you, then how can you contend with the horses?* (i.e. *If you think it's hard now...*)

God's question of Elijah reflects upon the man's entire career as a prophet: "What are you doing here (in this cave)?" God has brought Elijah to a point where He can work things out and regain his passion. **What is God asking of you right now?**

A Loaded Answer

Elijah's response is from the heart—and that's the problem! His answer is filtered through the heart of man and not the heart of God. Let's read:

> *"So he (Elijah) said, 'I have been very zealous for the Lord God of hosts; for the children of Israel have forsaken Your covenant, torn down Your altars, and killed Your prophets with the sword. I alone am left; and they seek to take my life'"* I Kings 19:10.

The response is one of frustration and self-pity and follows a typically human attitude anchored in pride:

Defensive: *I have been doing a great job for you, Lord!*
Judgmental: *Everyone else is doing a sorry job for you, Lord!*

How often the people of God cry, "Foul!", and point fingers when the answer to their frustration centers in their attitude and exercise of faith. Pacesetters must constantly evaluate themselves in light of God's truth.

The Lord tells Elijah to meet Him outside of the cave on the mountain. As God moved closer the elements reacted as the mountain shook and the winds drove fiercely into the rocks. Elijah moved to the entrance of the cave and the Lord asked him again, "What are you doing here?" Again, Elijah defends his record of zealousness and points out that he is very much alone in all this. The Lord responds differently:

> *"Then the Lord said to him, "Go, return on your way to the wilderness of Damascus..."* I Kings 19:15.

The solution to all of Elijah's fears and frustrations are found in the simple admonition to recover that which has been given up; to return to God as we first came to Him. Three simple steps can help us to recover our passion for the Lord and become on fire for Him once again:

1. Faith in God to lead us in triumph.
2. Trust in God to keep us from harm.
3. Love for God which motivates our ministry.

The Lord also reminds Elijah that there are seven thousand faithful in Israel apart from him who have not worshipped other gods. Elijah is not as alone as he suspected (I Kings 19:18). We must:

C. Realize there are other people on fire for God.

Finally, as an act of encouragement for the recovering prophet, God brings Elisha into Elijah's ministry to be apprenticed as a future prophet and to share in the work of the ministry to Israel. (I Kings 19:19-21)

D. We need a partner to walk with us and encourage us.

Elijah's passion was restored and he continued on in service to the Lord until God actually removed him from the earth and took him into heaven. So great was his passion, that when Elisha inherited the office he asked the Lord for a double portion of the Spirit which had been on Elijah.

The key to Elijah's return to a passionate ministry was found in standing in the Lord's presence. It was only when Elijah emptied himself that God was able to begin the recovery. We must be willing to empty ourselves of the prideful attitudes which seek to bring us down, and make us feel the need to defend our records and point our fingers. **Passion *for* God is born out of relationship *with* God. Remember, passion without relationship is emotion; relationship without passion is religion.** Let's go after the real thing!

---

1. Ray Comfort, <u>Militant Evangelism</u>, (New Zealand: Living Waters Publications, 1985), p. 51.

Chapter Eleven

Passionate Prayer: The Pulse of a Pacesetter

> *"More things are wrought by prayer than this world dreams of. Wherefore, let thy voice rise like a fountain for me night and day. For what are men better than sheep or goats that nourish a blind life within the brain, if, knowing God, they lift not hands of prayer both for themselves and those who call them friend? For so the whole round earth is every way bound by gold chains about the feet of God."[1]*
>
> Alfred Lord Tennyson

Prayer. The very word evokes a number of ideas to everyone. To some it means a time alone with God for solace and instruction; for others it is a few phrases that are said at meals and before turning in for the night. Many find prayer to be a transforming experience, while others view it a slippery prospect that is difficult to cultivate personally. To the Pacesetter, however, prayer is the very pulse of passion. It is the essence of relationship with the Father from which flows His goodness and power for ministry to a lost world.

True prayer and true passion go hand in hand. Our best example of the coupling of these two essential ingredients for success in life is Jesus. Here was a man (who was also fully God) who understood the need for personal times of prayer with the Father. He would often seek a place of prayer, even when He was very tired from a long day of ministry. Yet, Jesus knew that in order to carry out the Father's plan of redemption, He must include time spent with the Father as a part of the routine. As Christians, we too have a plan of redemption to carry out and it must be bathed in prayer as well.

In the last chapter I discussed the possibilities of passion: gaining, losing and regaining a real passion for the Lord as it related to the prophet Elijah. But as I have already stated, passion and prayer go together. In this chapter we're going to examine the praying side of the prophet and how his life of passion was built upon his life of prayer and the ability to believe God for great things when he did pray...and how God will do the same for us! But let's look at...

Four Types of Prayer

In the book of James we are given a section of scripture dealing with prayer and the different types of prayer accessible to Christians. James writes:

"Is anyone among you suffering? Let him pray. Is anyone cheerful? Let him sing psalms.

Is anyone among you sick? Let him call for the elders of the church, and let them pray over him, anointing him with oil in the name of the Lord.

And the prayer of faith will save the sick, and the Lord will raise him up. And if he has committed sins, he will be forgiven.

Confess your trespasses to one another, and pray for one another, that you may be healed. The effective, fervent prayer of a righteous man avails much.

Elijah was a man with a nature like ours, and he prayed earnestly that it would not rain; and it did not rain on the land for three years and six months.

And he prayed again, and the heaven gave rain, and the earth produced its fruit." James 5:13-18.

I.   Personal Prayer:

"Is any one of you in trouble? He should pray." (v.13) God is very understanding of personal needs, if He wasn't, He would not make the provision for bringing personal needs to Him. He knows that our limited human condition is fraught with the troubles of life. Jesus encourages us with the words, ***"In the world you will have tribulation, but be of good cheer: I have overcome the world." (John 16:33)*** In the big-picture perspective, the solution to our worldly dilemmas is to focus in on Jesus who blazed an overcoming trail for us. However, God is sympathetic with the small picture and knows that we don't live "in the sweet by and by" yet, and invites us to bring personal needs to Him. Because of this fact, we may approach God boldly whenever we are in trouble or despair. He will not turn us away.

Notice the emphasis in the verse is on **"you."** Is any of "<u>you</u>" in trouble? God places a premium on the individual because in working His will through individuals He is working His plan throughout the entire Body of Christ. We need not feel guilty about bringing personal situations to God;

but we must be careful what we promise God in moments of desperation: "God, if you get me out of this mess I'll become a preacher." Fox-hole prayers can be dangerous! The point of personal prayer is that we must be willing to approach the Father in our time of need. We are responsible to come to Him in faith.

II. Corporate Prayer

"...he should call for the elders" (v. 14) Again the responsibility is on the individual to bring the matter before the Lord, and for the individual to call the church and let the elders know that he or she is sick and needs prayer. Corporate prayer recognizes our dependence upon one another and the need to bear each other's burdens. It is not that the Lord cannot heal in a private setting, but by bringing a matter before the elders there is a sense of community and shared ministry which helps build the unity of the church. People who see a praying eldership will have more confidence in the leadership of the church and the ministry it is bringing forth. The church is nothing if it is not a community of believers caring for one another. Paul speaks of the Church as an organism, a body with many parts, each important to the whole. Of this body he writes:

> "And if one member suffers, all the members suffer with it; or if one member is honored, all the members rejoice with it" I Corinthians 12:26.

Corporate prayer stimulates the life of the Body by demonstrating shared concern and care for the individuals within the group. The result is confidence in God's structured leadership and in His methodology.

III. Partner Prayer

"Therefore confess your sins to each other and pray for each other that you may be healed" (v. 16) What a special bond is created when two Christians pray in confidence for each other. It is God's desire that we have someone with whom we can confide our deepest needs and dreams; someone who will believe with us and for us; someone who will not shame us in our sins nor scoff at our desires.

Partner Prayer is a prayer of intimacy and disclosure. Why? Because it is predicated upon the ability to confess to each other those things which are sinful in order to begin walking in integrity. The ability to confess, whether to our heavenly Father or to a brother or sister in the Lord, is paramount to recovery from sin and the guilt it brings.

Proverbs 28:13 says, *"He who conceals his sins does not prosper, but whoever confesses and renounces them finds mercy." (NIV)* By openly admitting a sin we struggle with, we are disarming its ability to control us. Why? Because when darkness is exposed it must flee—sometimes with a fight—but light is the beginning of the end for darkness. Notice also that the proverb instructs us not only to confess our sin but also to renounce it. That means we must admit our sin and deal with it through repentance and taking action to avoid falling to it again. This is critical because our ability to have passionate prayer is hindered when we are openly sinning:

> *"But your iniquities have separated you from your God; and your sins have hidden His face from you, so that He will not hear"* Isaiah 59:2.

When we continue in our sins, God refuses to listen to our prayers. He cannot hear what we are saying because He can see what we are doing! Does that mean we must be perfect for God to hear our cries to Him? Of course not—

otherwise none of us would have ever been saved when we cried out to Him in an unregenerate condition. **The principle is that God is Holy and will not tolerate a sinful lifestyle which presumes to call upon Him as if everything was OK.**

Sin is never OK.

God, being the gracious Person He is, has determined that if we confess and repent of our sins, He will respond with mercy and renewed relationship. Our hope is in our confession. *We should never pass up an opportunity to repent of sin* because the reward can change the course of an individual's life—even the life of an entire nation:

> *"If my people who are called by My name will humble themselves, and pray and seek My face, and turn from their wicked ways, then I will hear from heaven, and will forgive their sin and will heal their land"* II Chronicles 7:14.

If only the Christians would get it right, our country would be in position to receive God's blessing. He promises to cover an entire nation, wicked and righteous alike, for the sake of those who love Him. **When the United States has more Pacesetters instead of trend followers, we will be on the road to revival and blessing.** God is calling upon all Christians to become Pacesetters and start establishing a standard of excellence for God in their schools, churches, businesses and homes. He *wants* to bless; but His hands are tied by His own people's lack of humility and unwillingness to confess and renounce sin.

IV. Passionate Prayer

"The effectual fervent prayer of a righteous man availeth much." *(v 16) KJV* This type of prayer brings us to Elijah. Effective, fervent and passionate prayer was Elijah's method.

It had to be! Elijah was aware, that apart from the miraculous in an unforgiving and skeptical world, his ministry was finished. But God rewarded his fervency as we will shortly see.

What is *effectual* and *fervent?* **To effect means literally to "bring to pass" or "to accomplish."** To be effectual means "to have the ability to produce or accomplish something." The word "fervent" is related to the word "fever" and means "to glow, boil or rage." The idea is one of great activity, like boiling water in a pot, restless and hot. To be fervent is "to demonstrate great strength of passion and intensity, a boiling inside."

To be fervent and effectual means that a person is intense in their prayers, raging inside with passion so that they may effect, through God, a desired or needed outcome. This is the type of prayer that shakes demonic strongholds; that demolishes principalities and powers; that delivers from darkness and moves heaven and earth. This is the kind of prayer Elijah lifted up to the Lord during his ministry.

One of the most comforting truths about serving God is the fact that God uses ordinary people to do extraordinary things. People like you and me and the guy sitting next to you in the pew have all the potential of God vested within our hearts. Unless a person is in some way disabled physically, emotionally or mentally, anyone has the ability to believe God for great things and see Him perform the miraculous. Elijah was such a man.

"Elijah was a man just like us..." James writes that Elijah was a normal person, with normal problems. He had no greater advantage, as he grew in the Lord than anyone of us today, yet God used him mightily. He was human, and struggled with all the issues with which humans must deal: sickness, fear, temptation, etc. He was not a perfect man. Yet, God enabled him to become one of the greatest figures in the Bible. How? I believe that Elijah's strength centered

on his devotion to God through prayer. **And our success or failure in ministry can be directly related to the quality of our prayer life.** Prayer encompasses every aspect of the Christian life because it is our vital link with the Father. In *The Power and the Blessing*, Jack Hayford puts it this way:

> *"Whatever else may be said about either living as a disciple of Jesus Christ or walking with Him by faith, in love, through trial and in power, prayer is the one discipline above and beneath all others...The Bible's call to prayer is not a call to the mystical or to the theoretical. The pathway to prayer is preeminently learnable, not intended to be mysterious, and always intended to be practical."[2]*

"He prayed earnestly..." Elijah didn't pray a half-hearted petition to God with a vague, "if it be your will, O Lord," attached to the end. No! He prayed with fervency, earnestly and with passion. He knew that those effects which are the greatest and most significant, require the most extreme and dedicated prayers of faith. He was intense as he cried out to God, and God responded accordingly, bringing far-reaching repercussions not only to Elijah personally, but all of Israel:

For Elijah: A greater sense of confidence in his ability to move God's heart was born which would serve him later at Mt. Carmel against the Baal prophets.

For Israel: They saw the power of God demonstrated and were reminded that He is Lord of heaven *and* earth.

God is looking not only for people who will change the world, but who will, in the process, become changed themselves. His interest is in what He is producing rather than the means by which something is produced. So, how can we tell whether or not our prayer is earnest? **If we are being changed ourselves.**

Many times I have often been in deep prayer seeking the face of God. It is in these times that the Holy Spirit will often begin to do a deep work within me. I have not intentionally begun my prayer times with myself as the focus, but the Lord has changed me during these prayer times. It is like the prophet Isaiah who begins to have a vision of God. He realizes that he needs to change himself and then God will bring a change to the people he is ministering to. Again if our prayer is earnest and fervent we will be changed by it ourselves.

Elijah's Prayer

"And Elijah the Tishbite, of the inhabitants of Gilead, said to Ahab, 'As the Lord God of Israel lives, before whom I stand, there shall not be dew nor rain these years, except at my word'" I Kings 17:1.

Elijah didn't waste any words or time when it came to asking God for what he wanted to see happen. He knew that if the Lord withheld rain, the people would finally cry out to God to deliver them. He prayed with confidence that God would do precisely as he requested. The key to Elijah's confidence rested not on who he *was*, but who the Lord *is*. This all goes back to the first chapter on knowing God personally.

Our confidence is in the Lord. He is the one who will perfect that which concerns us. Paul wrote to the Philippians that the Lord, who began a good work within us would faithfully complete the task (Phil. 1:6). The burden for completion of a work in our life is on the Lord, not us. It is He who will be faithful to complete whatever He has started. We need only give Him room to operate. Proverbs 3:36 says that *"the Lord shall be your confidence."* If God is our confidence, how can we possibly doubt?

So it is, that Elijah can say with confidence that the Lord "before whom I stand" will fulfill that very thing for which he will pray. Here is what one commentator writes:

> *"In I Kings 1:17 we read: 'As the Lord the God of Israel lives, before whom I stand, there shall be neither dew nor rain these years, except by my word.' Now the Jewish attitude of prayer was standing before God; and so in the phrase the Rabbis found what was to them an indication that the drought, was the result of the prayers of Elijah. In I Kings 18:42 we read that Elijah went up to Mt. Carmel, bowed himself down upon the earth and put his face between his knees. Once again the Rabbis saw the attitude of agonizing prayer; and so found what was to them an indication that it was the prayer of Elijah which brought the drought to an end."*[3]

> *"And it came to pass after many days that the word of the Lord came to Elijah, in the third year, saying, 'Go, present yourself to Ahab, and I will send rain on the earth'"* I Kings 18:1.

After three-and-one-half years of no rain, God finally comes back to Elijah and tells him to tell the king of Israel that the drought will end soon. Notice that the drought ended upon the word of the Lord coming to Elijah. What Elijah had set in motion by faith, God was bringing to a close in His perfect timing. We must allow God the maximum benefit of time to work His will. If we try to jump out ahead of the plan, we will only further delay things or become increasingly frustrated. Chances are that at some point during that drought, Elijah prayed to God to go ahead and let it rain; after all, he was effected by lack of water too! But we must allow God's fullness of time to be expressed. Jesus didn't come until just the right time, though people had been looking for Him for centuries.

Not Just His Rain, But His Reign

Whenever we read about rain (or lack thereof) in the Bible, we need to examine the larger context and determine if there is another meaning the Lord is symbolically teaching us. Rains often symbolizes revival, not only physical restoration of a parched earth, but spiritual renewal of a parched spirit. The prophet Joel spoke on this subject:

> *"And it shall come to pass afterward that I will pour out My Spirit on all flesh; your sons and your daughters shall prophesy, your old men shall dream dreams, your young men shall see visions.*
> *And also on My menservants and on My maidservants I will pour out My Spirit in those days"* Joel 2:28-29.

Rain brings revival. The idea Joel is expressing is that God will pour forth His Spirit upon His weary servants, that they may do great exploits in the latter days. The latter days refers to the time just before Jesus returns for His people. Like rain, God is pouring out His Spirit upon all people; but in particular, His servants are the ones who will receive and understand its significance. How gracious of our Lord to generously pour His Spirit upon everyone equally—all people, good and bad alike—though only His servants will be blessed. God wants everyone who is receptive to be blessed. If the wicked repent and receive His Spirit which is being poured out upon them, they too will have dreams and visions.

Rain brings refreshing. Just as the rain refreshes the earth after a long dry season, so are God's people refreshed whenever He pours His Spirit into us. Rain brings forth new life and rekindles the old life. God causes it to rain on both the just and the unjust because He loves all people. But the real refreshing can only be received by those in relationship with God.

Remember the woman at the well talking with Jesus in John 4? She wanted to be refreshed with water. Jesus told her that the water she was seeking would only refresh her for a little while, but He could offer water which would produce eternal benefits. Let's not just pray for His rain; let's be praying for His reign!

Just as there are ways to promote and receive God's reign in our life, there are ways to stop it as well: *sin*. If we are continuing in sin as individuals or as a people, we will stop the flow of God's refreshing rain in our lives. True, God pours His Spirit out on all flesh. But if we are in sin, we will not be able to perceive God's Spirit being poured out. Sin short-circuits our ability to receive from God and His ability to hear from us.

This principle of maintaining a right relationship and living up to covenant responsibilities runs the course of the Bible. We have an "if...then" relationship with God: *If* we live according to His word, *then* we will be blessed. *If* we live not according to His word, *then* we will not be blessed. Simple, but devastating, if one cannot break a sin cycle in his life. If you don't believe me, take a look at Deuteronomy 28. But didn't Jesus do away with all that and bring grace into the picture? Yes, but remember that Jesus came to fulfill the Old Testament, not to abolish it. He brings a greater expression of the Spirit behind what was written in the days of Moses so that although we live under grace, we are still held accountable for our actions. The wages of sin is still death!

Moving God's Hand

In His Sermon on the Mount, Jesus told us that we are to be persistent with the Lord. We are to ask, seek and knock that the doors of opportunity and blessing might be opened to us. God invites us to approach Him in prayer so that He might move in our behalf. What moves God's hand? Prayer. Praying and crying out to God brings deliverance. We see this time and time again throughout scripture. In Exodus 3, God responds to the crying of His people by sending them a deliverer in the form of Moses. In Judges, God sends men and women of God to deliver the Jews from different oppressors. God responds to the heartfelt cries of His people.

When Elijah prayed for the rain to return after he received word from the Lord that the drought would end soon, God opened up the heavens and brought forth rain. Look at Elijah's attitude as he prayed:

> "...And Elijah went up to the top of Carmel; then he bowed down on the ground, and put his face between his knees, and said to his servant, 'Get up now, look toward the sea.' So he went up and looked, and said, 'There is nothing.' And seven times he said, 'Go again.'
>
> Then it came to pass the seventh time, that he said, 'There is a cloud, as small as a man's hand, rising out of the sea!'" I Kings 18:42-22.

Elijah exhibits three attitudes in this prayer:

1. Persistence. Though it took seven times, Elijah would have been content for it to have taken 70 times 7, if necessary. He knew that God would be true to His Word and persevered until the results came about. Are you willing to wait it out—even if it seems to delay endlessly?

163

2. Humility. Elijah humbled himself before the Lord, both in physical posture and in attitude. He knew that unless God acted he would never see the rain. We need to remember that we are at God's mercy as to whether or not He will act in our behalf. We know He will because He said He would, but He is a sovereign Lord over whom we have no control. *"I will have mercy on whom I have mercy, and compassion on whom I have compassion." (Exodus 33:19) NIV*

3. Anticipation. Elijah didn't simply pray and wait to see how things turned out. He looked for the answer. He searched it out because he was devoted to seeing God's response. This is a real demonstration of faith on the part of Elijah. He could have prayed for rain and waited for the Lord to answer in some casual way. No, Elijah was intense and waited with open eyes to see the answer from God. We must develop that sort of vigilant attitude in prayer; a Ph.D of prayer:

> **P**ersistence
> **H**umility
> **D**evotion

Jesus is our greatest example of the importance of prayer in the life of a Pacesetter. Reread the gospels and you'll find our Lord spends much time in prayer. He told us that we must be vigilant in prayer, we must have our Ph.D. in prayer down. In Luke 18 Jesus told a parable about a woman who persistently knocked on the door of a judge trying to get him to see things her way. Finally, in exasperation, he gave in to her simply to get rid of her. Now God does not desire to get rid of us, but he does invite us to be persistent with Him. The point of the parable is introduced in Luke 18:1, *"Then Jesus told his disciples a parable to show them that they should always pray and not give up."* Persistence in prayer is paramount!

Summing It Up

How does God view your prayer life right now? Is He happy with it? Does it need some attention? Chances are all of us can do a better job of praying. If we are to be the Pacesetters this world needs, we must begin by having a revival in our own prayer lives. How can we instruct others in the things of God if we ourselves are not in constant communication with Him? Here are some ideas of what we all should be working out in our prayer lives:

1. Ask God for a passion for prayer. The Bible says that God will give us the desires of our hearts. If your desire is to become a man or woman of prayer, ask God to help you in that endeavor. Get around other Christians who have a great prayer life and ask them to disciple you. Whatever you do, be persistent!

2. Make a list of people for whom you can pray. One of the best ways to begin a life of prayer is to have something to pray about regularly. Ask God to give you people to pray for. List them out and pray with them all the time. You'll be amazed as God begins to work in their lives according to your prayers!

3. Make a decision not to give up praying. If you're like most Christians, you've probably made the decision before to pray every day for such and such amount of time. After a while, the schedule began to fall apart and soon you found yourself not praying at all. The key is to pray...period! Make up your mind that you will pray everyday no matter what. Don't even worry about a set amount of time yet. Allow God to develop those details. Just concentrate on developing the habit of prayer.

4. Pray for your community. We are to be salt and light to a lost world. This includes your neighborhood, school, church, place of employment, etc. Your energies spent in ministry to these areas will go much farther if you have spent some time previously in prayer to "soften up" the beaches before you make a landing. Call it a preemptive strike on enemy territory! And pray!

5. Pray for the rain. Pray that the Spirit of God will be poured out over your life and the lives of those Christians around you who are ministering servants of God. Our world is desperate for something positive to happen. Only the Spirit of God can bring about true peace and fulfillment to a distressed planet.

I close this chapter with a reading from Hebrews which clearly illustrates that Jesus had persistence, humility and devotion when He prayed:

> *"who, in the days of His flesh, when He had offered up prayers and supplications, with vehement cries and tears to Him who was able to save Him from death, and was heard because of His godly fear,"* Hebrews 5:7.

May all of us develop the kind of life which enables the Lord to hear our prayers because of reverent submission to Him.

Pacesetters—Be passionate in prayer!

---

1. From a poem by Alfred Lord Tennyson
2. Jack Hayford, The Power and the Blessing, (Wheaton: Victor Books, 1994), p. 169.
3. William Barclay, The Letter of James and Peter, (Philadelphia: The Westminster Press, 1976), p. 132.

Chapter Twelve

The Standard

> *"Did you ever see a bush burn, and yet not be consumed? Did you ever see a spark float in the sea, and yet not be quenched? Many persons here are, to themselves, just such wonders. They are living godly lives in the midst of temptation, holy in the midst of impurity, serving God in spite of all opposition."*[1]
>
> From "2200 Quotations from the Writing of Charles H. Spurgeon," compiled by Tom Carter

We have seen throughout this book the principles that make one a Pacesetter. In this final chapter, I want to end with the simple challenge for all of us to set a standard for others to follow. This challenge must not be merely taken as an intellectual assent, but must be taken deep within our hearts. Unless something makes its way deep into our hearts then all one possesses is more head knowledge. The world is filled with people who know the right things, but it is time to buck the trend of just knowing and go to the doing stage.

The Apostle Paul gives us some important traits of a person who wants to set a standard:

> *"But what things were gain to me, these I have counted loss for Christ. Yet indeed I also count all things loss for the excellence of the knowledge of Christ Jesus my Lord, for whom I have suffered the loss of all things, and count them as rubbish, that I may gain Christ"* Philippians 3:4.

1. Paul needed a heart experience.

Paul was a man who had a lot of head knowledge in religion. He was one who was highly educated in knowing all the ins and outs of the religion of the day. However, Paul makes it clear that the only thing that is worth anything is knowing Christ. The word, "know," in the Greek is not just intellectual, but it is talking about an intimate relationship with Jesus. In other words, Paul is saying that it is a heart relationship that he not only has but is desiring even more of. Oh, I hope that is the cry of your heart! That everything is considered nothing in comparison to knowing Christ. Wuest in his word study book says, "The expression 'the knowledge of Christ Jesus my Lord,' does not refer to the knowledge which the Lord Jesus possesses, but the knowledge of the Lord Jesus which Paul gained through the experience of intimate companionship and communion with Him."[2]

2. Paul had the desire within.

Paul goes on to state further in the chapter what he really wanted:

> *"...that I may know Him and the power of His resurrection, and the fellowship of His sufferings, being conformed to His death,"* Philippians 3:10.

You see Paul had the desire within himself. Again he made it clear that he wants to know Christ. The term implies to know intimately by experience, to understand.[3] Paul had an inner desire to seek God and not to be satisfied. The trend would have been to relax and enjoy all that he knows, but Paul was a Pacesetter who was setting the standard.

Paul also made it clear that it was a personal desire that possessed him. He says I want to know Christ. In order to set the standard for others we must have a personal desire to go after Christ. It cannot be the desire of your pastor, parent, peers or spouse. The desire must be your own birthed in your heart by the Holy Spirit. It reminds me of when I decided to get serious about knowing Christ for myself. The Lord impressed upon my heart to spend Friday and Saturday nights seeking Him and preparing sermons. So off I went to the chapel of the church I used to attend in Whittier, California. I would show up, pray and preach for three hours on Friday, and spend time seeking God on Saturday. It was during these months that I began to know God for myself. Nobody was pushing me or telling me, the desire came from within me. As Pacesetters, we need to continually ask the Lord for the desire to burn in us on a daily basis. Nobody can give you the desire, only the Holy Spirit.

3. Paul had the power from without.

Paul states that he wants to know the power of Christ's resurrection. The term, "power," comes from the Greek word, "dunamis." The definition includes miraculous power, ability, might, strength for a mighty work. Paul realizes that God has given us the power from without to deposit within us the ability to accomplish great things. God has given us the power found in the resurrection of Jesus—the promised Holy Spirit! God has given us power:

1) Over the enemy (1 John 4:4),
2) To witness (Acts 1:8),
3) Over sin (Romans 6:6-11),
4) To give us life (Romans 8:11).

Paul makes it clear that we are not living in the world powerless, but have been given a deposit of the Holy Spirit! Remember, God has given us the power from without and deposited it within to help us set the standard for others to follow.

4. Paul possessed perseverance.
Paul writes and tells us:

"Not that I have already attained, or am already perfected; but I press on, that I may lay hold of that for which Christ Jesus has also laid hold of me" Phillipians 3:12.

Paul knew that he was on a journey and that his destination was heaven! Notice that Paul makes it clear that he has not arrived and he is certainly not a perfect man. This man knew that in and of himself there was nothing to be liked or wanted. It was only his desire to be like Christ that accounted for anything. You see, God is not looking for perfect people, but people of perseverance. I like to say that we need to be people who are go-getters and not quitters! As a Pacesetter, remember that setting the standard takes perseverance to accomplish all that God has for you.

Paul goes on to say that he presses on to take hold of that which Christ has taken hold of him. Paul uses the word, press, which means to force your way forward, to push through. Paul wants to take hold of the things of God because the things of God have taken hold of him. But he knows that he must press past the barriers in order to become all that God wants him to be. Paul realizes that in order to be a Pacesetter he must yield his whole self to God and not allow the barriers of self or other people's opinions to stop what God wants to accomplish in his life.

5. Paul let go of the past.

Paul goes on to show us some more keys to being a Pacesetter in the day in which we live:

"Brethren, I do not count myself to have apprehended; but one thing I do, forgetting those things which are behind and reaching forward to those things which are ahead," Philippians 3:13.

Notice what Paul says the one thing he does. Paul could have done many different things, but he chose to focus in on one thing—forgetting what is behind. In order to be Pacesetters, we need to be people who leave the past in the past. The trend is to dig up the past and rehash it over and over. I believe that we need to look at the past, deal with it, get healing from it, and go on. I remember one person telling me that you cannot drive a car looking in the rear view mirror. Paul is exhorting us to let go of the past both the defeats and the victories. In order to set the standard, we must let go of the past and not deny it, but get healed from it and go on.

I have heard people telling me how they cannot do anything with their lives because of what has happened to them. I tell them that the past does not have to hold you back from your future. Our past hurts or failures can either be stepping stones or tombstones. Your past will be something to build on or it will bury you. The choice is left up to you and me and what will we decide. Let us not follow the trend of blaming all of our problems on what has happened. We need to hear what God says, forget the past and move on to the present, and look forward to the future. It reminds me of sport teams that suffer a loss. The team has a decision to make; it is either going to learn from the mistakes or dwell on them. If the team learns and corrects the mistakes, chances are that they, hopefully, win the upcoming game. However, wallowing in the failure and reliving it will only bring defeat in the future.

Paul goes on to say that he is reaching forward or straining to what is ahead. This is a picture of a runner who is setting the pace by straining every muscle in his body as he nears the finish line. In order to set the standard, our energy must be focused forward and not focused on the failure in the past. **The key is know that the best days for you and me are not behind us but ahead of us.** Only in the future can we know God better and accomplish great things for Him. The trend of looking in the past will only kill the vision of what God has for us in the future. Remember, the destiny that God has for you and me is always ahead of us and never behind us. Eventually, all of us will reach heaven which is in the future for all of us.

5. Paul knew his final destination and high calling.

Paul knew that his final destination was not wrapped up in this earth. Notice the following verse:

"I press toward the goal for the prize of the upward call of God in Christ Jesus" Philippians 3:14.

Paul makes it clear that again he is pressing with all his might to reach the mark for the prize of the high calling. Everyone of us have a high calling. As Pacesetters, we need to realize the extent of the call and strive to go after it with all our might. Our high calling causes us to have commitment in our Christian walk and not to be casual. The word commitment is not a word many Christians relish or even like to hear. But in order to "Set the Standard and Not Follow the Trend," we need to have a determination and commitment to our walk with Christ. Charles Spurgeon, one of the greatest preachers to ever live, once said, *"I wish that saints would cling to Christ half as earnestly as sinners cling to the devil. If we were willing to suffer for God as some are to suffer for their lusts, what perseverance and zeal would be seen on all sides!"[4]* May new Pacesetters be raised up in America today and may you be one of them!

6. Finally Paul wanted to be an example.

Paul makes it clear that he was a Pacesetter in his day and that people could follow his example:

> *"Brethren, join in following my example, and note those who so walk, as you have us for a pattern"* Philippians 3:17.

It is interesting to note that Paul was confident that he was doing his best in following the Lord. His life was an example for others to follow and imitate. This is what the Lord is calling for us to do once again. We are called to raise the standard so that others may follow in our footsteps. No longer can we wallow in mediocrity and low living. The clarion call of a Pacesetter is being heard across our land and world. People are no longer looking to be normal, but they want more out of life than news, weather, and sports.

The world has had Pacesetters that we could emulate. Look at Billy Graham, the man of utmost character and integrity. He is a Pacesetter that many have patterned their life after. However, Billy Graham will pass off of the scene

173

and God will raise up other men and women to be examples for the next generation. Will you join me and many others who will Set the Standard for this generation? What are you waiting for? Time is short and the need is great. You have everything in order to make it, but you must make the decision to go for it. Let's go for it Pacesetters! The world is tired of the same old trends and is looking those who will **SET THE STANDARD!**

1. Tom Carter, *compiler*, 2200 Quotations from the Writings of Charles H. Spurgeon, (Grand Rapids: Baker Books, 1988), p.101.

2. Kenneth S. Wuest, Wuest's Word Studies, (Grand Rapids: Wm. B. Eerdmans Publishing Company,), p. 91.

3. James Strong, LL.D., S.T.D., The New Strong's Exhaustive Concordance of the Bible, (Nashville: Thomas Nelson Publishers, 1990).

4. Carter, p. 35.

To order additional copies of

**Pacesetters:
Setting the Standard, Not Following the Trend**

please send your donation of $10.00 or more
for each book to:

*Pacesetters International
4705 Grove Street
Marysville, WA 98270*

Please add $4.00 shipping and handling for each book
requested and allow up to 4 weeks for delivery.

To order by phone, have your credit card ready and dial
1-800-917-BOOK

*Quantity Discounts Available

For additional products and tapes from
Pacesetters International write to the above address or
visit us on our website

http://www.pacesetters.org